256218 CONVERSATIONS WITH MICHAEL LANDON. By Tom Ito. A poignant tribute to the actor and director, interviews capturing his deepest thoughts and feelings are interspersed with personal recollections from his close friends and associates. Illus. 167 pages. Contemporary. Pub. at $16.95 **$2.95**

CONVERSATIONS WITH
MICHAEL LANDON

CONVERSATIONS WITH
MICHAEL LANDON

TOM ITO

CONTEMPORARY
BOOKS

CHICAGO

Library of Congress Cataloging-in-Publication Data

Ito, Tom.
    Conversations with Michael Landon / Tom Ito.
      p.   cm.
    ISBN 0-8092-3841-1 (cloth)
    1. Landon, Michael, 1936–1991.   2. Television actors and
actresses—United States—Biography.   3. Television
producers and directors—United States—
Biography.   I. Landon, Michael, 1936–1991.   II. Title.
PN2287.L2814I88   1992
791.45′028′092—dc20   92-25098
[B]   CIP

Published by Contemporary Books, Inc.
180 North Michigan Avenue, Chicago, Illinois 60601
Manufactured in the United States of America
International Standard Book Number: 0-8092-3841-1

For Michael: For memories . . .

"It was like the wellspring was close to the source . . . he had total confidence in what was within him to speak the truth, and it never let him down."

HARRY FLYNN
Michael Landon's longtime
friend and publicist

CONTENTS

FOREWORD

YOU ARE ABOUT TO EMBARK ON A WONDERFUL JOURNEY. In these pages you will get to know Michael Landon in the same way we who worked for and with him got to know him—through his own words and deeds.

In this volume, Michael gets to speak for himself. He talks about being the dreamer and helping others become dreamers. When Michael would retreat within himself, he was visiting a place without boundaries. This book takes you to that place. He taught us all that you can do and be whatever you dream, if you can only rid yourself of your inner limits.

It was almost a year after Michael's death before Tom Ito played for me some of the recordings of his interviews with Michael. Listening to Michael's casual, playful voice reminded me of the many paradoxes that were Michael

Landon. He was a man who was always searching . . . and always finding.

During my many years as Michael's production lawyer, he and I worked closely in a variety of situations, often under pressure. He had an easy way of expressing complete confidence in and loyalty to a person. He taught me a lot about how to achieve my own dreams, both personally and professionally. In these pages, you will learn why the men and the women and the children who were lucky enough to work with Michael Landon loved him so much.

Tom has a wonderful black-and-white photo of Michael, a copy of which appears in this book. Tom's copy is inscribed in Michael's familiar handwriting: "I feel I know myself better after you interviewed me." You will feel the same way . . . about Michael and about yourself. Enjoy.

Michael C. Donaldson
Beverly Hills, California
June 1992

ACKNOWLEDGMENTS

THE AUTHOR WISHES TO EXPRESS HIS APPRECIATION TO the following people for their kind and generous assistance:

Robert Caspar, J. D. and Julie Daniel, Michael Donaldson, Maureen Flannigan, Tom Flannigan, Harry and Pamela Flynn, Peggy Jago, Barbara Lashenick, Jeff Learned, Adelaide Moore, Diane and Doug McClure, Jim Mote, Brianne Murphy, Lawrence Myers, Pamela Roylance, David and Eveline Semel, Gene Trindl, Elda Unger.

A special thanks to my editor, Nancy Crossman, whose faith in this book along with her perceptive professional guidance and encouragement helped make the endeavor a reality.

CONVERSATIONS WITH
MICHAEL LANDON

BEGINNINGS

"I believe that we can all make our own miracles."
MICHAEL LANDON

1
FLASHBACKS

THE JAVELIN IS A BIBLICAL WEAPON. IN THE HANDS OF A
righteous man it is a symbol of valor. For a youngster
named Eugene Orowitz growing up in New Jersey, it became the instrument of a lifelong declaration to fight the
tough odds against personal triumph.

Enthralled with a motion picture called *Samson and
Delilah*, the boy became convinced that his own strength
would grow with the length of his hair. He began lifting
weights and doing push-ups, and as his hair grew longer
he could feel his strength increase. Eventually the far cast
of his javelin won him a college scholarship. He relin-
quished the javelin then, fired with the new resolve of
professional ambition.

He changed his name to Michael Landon but did not
cut his hair.

For the next three decades he struggled and fought to
build a creative career in television entertainment and

became one of the most powerful and respected independent producers in the industry. At the height of his achievement he was stricken with a grave illness. With a defiant, unassailable dignity, and still long-haired, Michael Landon announced to the world that he had cancer.

In April 1991 Landon summoned a press conference at his Malibu home and with forthright calmness informed reporters and television viewers that he had been diagnosed as having inoperable cancer of the liver and pancreas. He then proceeded, with characteristic humor and courage, to do a series of rigorous push-ups, demonstrating to his guests a spirited resolve to fight his illness.

It was a gallant attempt to allay the fears and possible misconceptions of family, friends, and fans—fears that would be aggravated by the merciless tabloid sensationalism that he knew would follow. The drama of Landon's battle for life evoked tremendous prayerful support from the public and, in the end, a profound sense of loss.

Landon's valiant determination to beat his illness, I feel, was the affirmation of his own invincible spirituality. "I believe that we can all make our own miracles," he asserted publicly. "I'm still hoping to beat it." It seemed to have been Michael's way to instinctively embrace life with a kind of tenacious serenity. "Death's gonna have to do a lot of fighting to get me," he said in a *Life* magazine article. "Yes, the odds are bad, but I've fought bad odds before."

Michael had long been a potent and formidable contender in a richly complex life. By the time I met him—and in some measure, I feel, came to know him—much of the storminess of his professional striving had passed. "I'm

sure a hell of a lot more mellow now," he remarked dryly
to me one balmy afternoon in Malibu.

Our discussion that day was one of three personal
conversations I had with Michael Landon that began with
our first meeting at Lorimar Studio in the autumn of 1989
and continued for the next year and a half, until approxi-
mately six months before his death on July 1, 1991. The
thoughts, feelings, and philosophy contained in this volume were gleaned from those talks.

Despite the immense creative success he built on un-
wavering, tough professionalism and pragmatic business
savvy, Landon exhibited during our encounters—and
throughout his life—a fascinating duality of assertive hu-
mility. That unique nature continued to impel him to
challenge the external limitations of our world by turning
to the spirit within, where there are no limits.

"But while life lasts," Landon affirmed to his readers
in *Life*, "it's good to remember that death is coming, and it's
good that we don't know when. It keeps us alert, reminds
us to live while we have the chance." The acceptance of
death is not, of course, tantamount to a resignation from
life. And one could not, I feel, have known this man and
have failed to be impressed by his reverence for the totality
of life. There is, indeed, an element of heroism that inevitably responds to challenge with an exaltation that is
perhaps unbounded by either happiness or unhappiness.

Beyond the heroism of Michael Landon's final struggle endures a legacy. It is the inspired belief that living the
dream may perhaps be the true realization of our own
miracles.

*Dressed in jeans and a blue denim shirt, he easily
could have been mistaken for a grip except for that
unforgettable mane of hair.*

2

ROLE REHEARSAL

BIG ED'S IS GONE NOW, AND IN A WAY THAT IS A GREAT
shame. Main Street in Culver City will never be quite the
same without that seedy old saloon sitting on its corner.
Because of its small town, fifties look, the little avenue of
storefronts lying between Venice and Washington boulevards and terminating with the neon lights of Big Ed's was
a favorite location spot of Michael Landon Productions,
particularly for Landon's third television series, "Highway
to Heaven."

Culver City in its own way is as much a television
neighborhood as Hollywood. Nearby looms MGM studio,
where Michael had his production office. People who live
in the area, as I do, are pretty used to seeing city blocks
zoned off for location shoots. Consequently, the perimeter

of honey wagons—small mobile dressing rooms—I noticed by Big Ed's one summer evening back in 1986 didn't particularly surprise me.

Film crews attract curious spectators, and I was as susceptible as anyone. It was near dusk, and the onlookers were fewer than they otherwise might have been. Cables sprawled across the sidewalks and along the street. Cameras and lights, intriguing in their arcane functions, imparted a kind of surrealistic look to the trafficless boulevards as the exterior of a dilapidated saloon front now gleamed incongruously in a chrome-bright spotlight.

Suddenly the light clicked off and the crew began to disband. They appeared to be a pleasant and informal blue-collar kind of group, similar to the team members you might idly root for at a Saturday softball game at the park. They were also one of the most efficient and respected production groups in the television industry and a league often envied by outsiders. A young crew member in a flannel shirt lifted a hefty-looking item of equipment into a huge van emblazoned with large painted letters: Michael Landon Productions.

Landon himself stood off slightly detached from the activity, holding a cigarette and a coffee cup, whistling softly to himself. Dressed in jeans and a blue denim shirt, he easily could have been mistaken for a grip, except for that unforgettable mane of hair.

Filming having apparently ceased, the few suppertime spectators timidly crossed the street and went about their business. A couple of kids on skateboards recognized the television star and rolled by him grinning, venturing shy glances as they passed.

Landon appeared unperturbed, and I was intrigued by his poise. Amid the highly charged and exhilarating activity of this 150-person company, the boss was quietly reflecting over his coffee and cigarette as if in a reverie. A large, robust white-haired man approached him for a few words, and Landon's contemplative features broke into a responsive smile. The big man walked off, and Landon resumed his meditation.

About three years later I discovered that the congenial white-haired confidant was Michael's partner, Kent McCray. Kent's unfailing administrative competence in running the crew was in fact largely responsible for much of Michael's serenity on the set.

I had great respect for Landon. There was a mystique about the man that was ethereal and yet solid with earthly integrity. Imparted to his television work, that quality exalted its entertainment value. I was aware of his publicized scraps with intrusive members of the press, his declarative stands on social and political issues, and his vehement insistence on maintaining creative control over his own professional endeavors.

His varied career nearly spanned the history of television itself. Commercial TV broadcasting was a scant seventeen years old when Landon made his acting debut in 1956. The small screen itself may have been primitive during those early years, but the artistic quality of direction, acting, and writing, as Michael later asserted to me, were not. The fledgling actor fell utterly in love with the budding medium called TV. It was a pioneer devotion that would last a lifetime, and it is perhaps significant that Landon's enduring celebrity emerged in the ambitious frontier saga "Bonanza," the first television series to be filmed in full color at NBC.

"Bonanza" became one of the most successful westerns in television history. Set in the mid-1800s, the series related the struggles of the Cartwright family as they fought to hold and operate a sprawling one-thousand-square-mile Sierra ranch called the Ponderosa. Lorne Greene headed the cast as Ben Cartwright, the family patriarch, with Pernell Roberts portraying his eldest son, Adam, Dan Blocker the genial giant and middle son, "Hoss," and Michael Landon the youngest son, Little Joe. For well over a decade enthusiastic viewers tuned in to see the Cartwright family as they rode four abreast on horseback straight toward their audience to a spirited musical score written by Jay Livingston and Ray Evans.

The show also made a star out of Michael Landon. As Joe Cartwright he portrayed the most rebellious and romantic member of the Cartwright clan. Hot-tempered and high-spirited, his character was constantly embroiled in some form of mischief or dramatic dilemma.

This was perhaps not a great departure from the youngster's own defiantly energetic personality. Sparks had often flown from Landon's friction with members of the show. William Claxton, who directed several "Bonanza" episodes, recalled in a recent television interview the young actor's pugnaciousness and fondly characterized

Michael in those early days as "a brat." The brat, however, was to grow up on that show. He developed a devouring fascination for television production and an intense drive to master the creative techniques of both writing and directing.

Veteran crew members of "Bonanza" recall the staggering number of hours the young star eventually logged studying camera and editing techniques. Photographer Gene Trindl, who throughout most of his thirty-year career worked with Michael, remembers him as "loving everything he did regarding the business. He couldn't seem to get enough of it." Consuming drive and ambition, however—especially in Hollywood—can sometimes be a mine field. The false step, the wrong direction, can be devastating.

Fortunately the mighty channel of work through which Landon chose to direct his immense energies proved to be one of the most fruitful alignments in his life. By the time "Bonanza" had ended its fourteen-year run, he not only had refined his professional attitude and skills as an actor but had debuted as a writer and director on that show as well.

In 1974, scarcely months after the cancellation of "Bonanza," the former baby brother of the Cartwrights returned to the NBC primetime airwaves, this time as the father figure of his own frontier family. When Michael, as the pioneer farmer Charles Ingalls, pulled up his covered wagon in the opening title scenes of his next series, "Little House on the Prairie," he was also holding the reins as executive producer.

The show became a beloved piece of television Americana and an eye-opening showcase for Landon's gifts as a director and writer. Based on the popular children's books by Laura Ingalls Wilder, the show chronicled the girlhood memories of Laura Ingalls (played by Melissa Gilbert) growing up with her family in the Minnesota hamlet of Walnut Grove.

Even more impressive than the intrinsic production and entertainment values of "Little House" were the traditional values of family unity and individual integrity that the show reaffirmed in a generally cynical primetime climate.

The series lasted for nine years. Countless viewers who grew up with the show also had an opportunity to watch Landon himself mature into an artist ascending to the height of his creative power. His writing, acting, and directing talents harmonized into an intuitive potency that served as the consistent driving force for his entire company.

It was a phenomenal success story. As an obscure writer struggling with aspirations of my own, I found Michael's apparent integrity and resolute climb to success inspiring. Well, now it was early evening on Main Street in Culver City. The "Little House on the Prairie" hamlet of Walnut Grove seemed far away. But there, a few feet in front of me, stood the medium-sized man in blue denim and white sneakers whose persistent drive for self-realization I had rather subconsciously begun to emulate.

It was strange to see a high-profile media figure

standing alone on a common sidewalk, unsurrounded by press, fans, or crew. Even in this dimming light Landon was still wearing his sunglasses. Now he began to pace a little, with a newly lit cigarette and an intense expression on his face.

I wrestled with the thought of speaking to him and found myself in a dilemma of indecision. I looked across the street once again somewhat hesitantly. I had read articles describing how temperamental the man could be. Because I wanted to like Landon, I had discounted the accounts, but I had never had to test them.

With a tentative shrug, I took the few deliberate steps across the street. "Excuse me," I called, walking up to the man. Landon stopped his pacing and looked at me. "Yeah," he acknowledged. I could smell the tobacco smoke, but I couldn't see the man's eyes behind the sunglasses.

"I just wanted to tell you that I've enjoyed your work for a lot of years." That was it. Landon's features assumed a smile, and we shook hands. "Well, thank you, thank you very much." A moment later, he walked away whistling softly to himself.

I was impressed by the sense of quiet strength the man projected. It was more than the firmness of his handshake, more definite than the resonance of a trained voice. Those were externals. There was something about Landon's presence, later confirmed by our conversations, that suggested an inner rectitude tempered by a silent spirituality. It was a thing unspoken yet somehow perceptible.

I pondered as I walked the block and a half back to my

apartment. Suddenly a notion took hold and murmured itself into words: "One of these days," I mused, "I'm going to work with that man." Verbalized aloud, the suggestion seemed absurd, a ridiculous presumption. Even alone, I found myself embarrassed. Yet somehow the thought persisted.

Three years later "Highway to Heaven" concluded a five-year run, and Landon was busily embarking on a campaign to syndicate the series. During the interim I had begun a small desktop publishing company named Soul of the Sword and was circulating an entertainment quarterly called *Yesteryears* around the greater Los Angeles area. It was a modest newsprint periodical that featured primarily personality profiles of television and radio celebrities and subsisted mainly on local advertising.

We opened our first year of business by running theme issues of *Yesteryears* that focused on individual aspects of the entertainment industry with supporting feature articles. A radio issue was followed by a television western issue and then one spotlighting celebrity art. The format was pretty simple and straightforward. Although our circulation was modest, people in various studios and production offices where we distributed the paper were generally both receptive to and kindly supportive of our overtures.

As a kid of the first television generation I have a genuine love of the small screen and the people who work in the medium. Therefore, when our modest publication was launched in 1989, it presented a generally upbeat and positive image of the industry, in particular by running humanistic rather than exploitive profiles of those interviewed. *Yesteryears* highlighted mainly television's golden years through its first three decades but featured contemporary profiles and articles as well.

Our first little sixteen-page issue was scarcely off the press when I elatedly contacted Michael Landon's publicist, Harry Flynn. I had a product now and a few interviews with genuine talents under my belt. Would Mr. Landon consider granting an interview for the purpose of composing a Michael Landon Productions issue of the quarterly? Harry was then, as he has unfailingly been since that first telephone call, a kindly and forbearing gentleman.

Beleaguered as he was by the publicity demands made of his popular client, Harry nevertheless did one thing for which I will forever honor him. *He took me seriously.* After all, we were hardly *TV Guide.* Harry read our first issue, complimented our efforts, and encouraged our growth. Michael's schedule was crowded, he explained, but he gently agreed to consider his client's possible accessibility for the project.

Yesteryears flourished, eventually growing from sixteen to thirty-two pages. Thirty-two pages! We were getting fat, and the critics were being kind—or at least holding their fire. Three issues after my first conversation with Harry, I received the long-hoped-for call.

It was late autumn of 1989. Michael, Flynn informed me, would be working with his film editor for a few days at Lorimar Studio on his then-current project, a television feature film called *Where Pigeons Go to Die*, starring Art Carney. "It's a good place to see him," advised Harry. "He'll be in his element. How about eleven o'clock, this coming Thursday morning?"

Harry had kept his word. Both he and Michael, I was to learn, were very good at keeping promises. I felt both hopeful and prepared. Perhaps I was even on my way to keeping a certain promise to myself.

He was born Eugene Maurice Orowitz, in Forest Hills, New York, in 1936. Michael Landon was the professional name that he selected from a telephone book.

3
SAM'S SON

I STILL FIND MYSELF A LITTLE AMAZED THAT MICHAEL Landon agreed to our first interview at all. His work schedule had been frenetic for years, and he was looking forward to a prolonged period of rest and travel with his family. When "Highway" wrapped its final show, it concluded a series run of 115 episodes. This had been preceded by nearly a decade during which Landon had produced an astonishing 208 episodes of "Little House." For the first time since he began work on "Bonanza" in 1959, he was uncommitted to doing a television series.

He certainly didn't need whatever publicity our rookie publication might generate. I doubt if he was even aware of who I was or the nature of my intention. I sensed that Harry understood my aspiration, which was to create a family album for television, and he had given me a gracious plug, and Michael trusted his judgment. Yet in the final analysis Landon always made his own decisions. The simple truth of the matter was that he was giving me a break.

I decided to walk the six blocks from my home to the studio. The tools of my trade were modest and portable. They included simply a pocket tape recorder zipped into a leather portfolio along with a pen and a yellow legal pad upon which I had composed my questions. The legal pad was merely a prop to suggest the courtesy of research. By then I had pretty much learned Landon's personal and professional background by heart.

He was born Eugene Maurice Orowitz, in Forest Hills, New York, in 1936. Michael Landon was the professional name that he selected from a telephone book.

Landon's parents had apparently been an unhappy and incompatible couple owing in no small measure to their different religious backgrounds. His mother, Peggy O'Neill, had been an actress and was also, as Michael later said, an Irish Catholic who devoutly hated Jews. Unfortunately his dad, Eli Orowitz, happened to be a Jew who was not particularly fond of Catholics. This irreconcilable rift, along with his mother's harsh and (according to Michael) sometimes violent eccentricities, tongue lashings, and open ridicule of the boy, made for a miserable childhood.

Michael attributed much of the trauma he suffered in his childhood directly to his mother's erratic behavior. In an interview for *Redbook* magazine in 1987, Landon forthrightly recalled some of those incidents of appalling abuse:

"She was a stabber, a kicker, and a wacko. She was off her rocker. She was very abusive. My mother would sit on the sofa in her nightgown—she always wore her nightgown when she was upset—holding a Bible, asking God to kill me. . . ."

". . . But my mother was a wonderful person to people who didn't know her. I don't know how many times people have come up to me and said, 'Your mother was the sweetest!' When they tell me that, I think of the time she came after me with a knife while I was in my jockey shorts. I was jumping fences in front of the neighbors as I tried to escape."

His unhappy childhood would leave Michael with the desire to be a good father to his nine children (the result of three marriages) later in life.

He and his older sister, Evelyn, grew up in Collingswood, New Jersey. As a kid, Michael was a shy runt, given to secret heroic daydreams. By night, for a humiliating period, he was a bed wetter, an experience he drew on when he wrote and directed the 1976 television movie *The Loneliest Runner*.

Landon's response was to ally himself, alone and in his mind, with heroes and a hero's strength. He read comic books, and he went to the movies. In the dark sanctuary of a motion picture theater he first saw the epic story of Samson, the long-haired slayer of Philistines. Emulation of this warrior summoned personal strength and a measure of self-confidence born of athletic achievement. It was a rite of passage that kindled within him the passionate assertiveness to succeed, an affirmation that led him to win a scholarship to USC as a javelin thrower and one that remained with him throughout his life. Twenty years later, Landon would recall those early, difficult years in a television drama he wrote and produced called "Sam's Son."

At USC, however, Landon found himself disillusioned by a hostile social environment and eventually quit college.

This decision led indirectly to a small role in a motion picture at Warner Brothers. Acting proved to be a liberating experience for the youth who found that he was not shy when he was able to play another character. The realization crystallized a strong-willed commitment within him. He would become an actor.

More than three decades and three television series later, Michael Landon had become one of the most powerful men in television production. It had been a career filled with creative controversies, professional confrontations, and artistic rivalries. Much of this contention was the result of Landon's insistence upon controlling virtually every aspect of any production he undertook. The quintessential independent producer, he was often a maverick who would fight when he felt the need to assert, even to skeptical network superiors, the validity of his creative gut instincts. Critics and comrades had often clashed in the winds of partisanship as Landon's stature in the entertainment industry—both as a compelling, passionate artist and as a tough-minded and shrewd businessman—grew.

THE
CONVERSATIONS

"I found I was not shy when I was someone else."
MICHAEL LANDON

4

FIRST TAKES

I CROSSED VENICE BOULEVARD TO MAIN STREET AND hiked along the same avenue where Big Ed's had once stood as a sentinel landmark. Harry met me at the studio gate. He led the way to a series of vintage buildings on the north end of the lot that were painted an aging gunmetal gray.

We climbed a haggard set of steps to an open corridor that resembled the deck of a destroyer. These were the editing rooms, and conjecture over how many millions of miles of film had reeled through those ancient apartments over the years was staggering. Harry apparently shared similar thoughts. "I am utterly awed when I think about the history this place has seen," he remarked as we headed past several of the sun-blistered doors. A robust voice called out a bawdy greeting to Harry as we peered down the end of the corridor to see Landon standing, silhouetted in the sunlight against the door of his editing room, several feet away. Harry grinned with open pleasure and fired back a ready quip.

The sun relented a little as we approached, and I could see that Michael's physical appearance entirely matched the vigor of his voice. His hair was as uncropped as ever and somewhat unruly. Casually dressed in a coral-colored sleeveless sweatshirt and tan slacks, he seemed in splendid shape. The sense of quiet strength I remembered from our brief encounter a few years back was now vividly perceptible.

Harry introduced us, and Michael shook hands with that automatic ease that comes from countless professional introductions. He was courteous and controlled, and it seemed gratuitous to mention our fleeting encounter of 1986. Michael in turn introduced me to his film editor, Jerry Taylor, and two other crew members, who grinned informally and shook hands.

While Taylor continued working with a clattering moviola, Michael kept up a casual banter with his publicist regarding some plumbing problems plaguing the Malibu house his family had recently moved to. Open boxes of various snack crackers stood on the film shelves behind the moviola, and Harry, who I have since learned is an inveterate nosher, gratefully foraged a handful.

"Do you guys like peanut butter?" Michael held out a plastic sandwich bag, inviting us to help ourselves to some peanut butter–filled pretzels. It was a nice icebreaker and for a casual interval we all stood around sampling the snack. "These are great," Landon remarked. "I know my kids would love them."

After a few minutes Jerry Taylor politely excused himself and, with Harry, joined their two other colleagues in the adjacent room, leaving Michael and me to our interview. It is usually cramped in an editing room, and this one was no exception. There was one chair, which Michael let me have. Obligingly he clicked on my portable tape recorder, placed it on a nearby shelf, and stood close by.

It was the first of what was to be three revealing conversations. Michael, I soon learned, was one of those exceptional individuals who have remarkably good communication with themselves. He was at his best when he said his own lines from his own heart as, simply, Michael Landon.

~

In a "Highway to Heaven" episode, I recall a line delivered to your character, Jonathan, from a small boy that went something like "My dad used to say that dreams are where you're going and work is how you get there." Would you say that applied to your own personal beliefs?

LANDON: I think so, very much. You know, it's no good to have dreams if you don't bust a little bit to accomplish them. And when I say dreams, I mean just that. I don't mean expectations. I don't have expectations. Expectations in your life just lead to giant disappointments. Dreaming is one thing, and working towards the dream is one thing, but working with expectations in mind, I think, is very self-defeating.

Was there ever a particular point in your life when you actively declared your independence as an individual?

LANDON: Oh, I pretty well did that at nine years old. My father had quit his job because he'd started a mail-order business. And he was losing his ass, but he wouldn't go back to his boss and ask for his job back. For what people were making in those days, he had a pretty good job—but he wouldn't go. I took a bus down into Camden and talked to his boss. "You know," I told him, "this is the best guy you could ever have working for you," because my father was a very hard worker, dedicated to his work—even though it wasn't a great job for him because he was a creative guy at one time.

I said, "You're both losing out. My dad isn't going to come to you and ask for the job back. But if you would offer him the job, if you would tell him how much you miss him, you would get a great worker back, because he desperately needs the job. He's losing his buns. Just don't tell him that I said anything to you." And he did, and my dad went back to work for them. But I felt at that time that I was more grown up than my father, because I felt that my father had allowed his false pride to get in the way.

Was there a particular role model or a catalyst—an individual or an event—that inspired your aspirations of self-realization? I know that you have the talisman, the long hair . . .

LANDON: No. Because I was *such* a loner. I spent so much time alone as a kid. Out of my house—I had an unhappy house, and I found great comfort in being alone. I enjoyed being alone a great deal. I still do. As many kids as I have, I love solitary time. I love early, real early morning.

You can still dream then.

LANDON: Yeah! I used to have a cave that I dug near my house. And I'd put canned goods in it, all kinds of stuff that I'd save up, and I'd sit there and fantasize that I was all these different comic book characters, Green Lantern, and I was fighting the Nazis in my little hometown. Every comic book character—I wanted to be one of those guys.

TV Guide quoted you as saying, "I had to dream just to get myself out of Collingswood. I dreamt everything."

LANDON: That quote really dealt with when I started to throw the javelin and realized that there was a possibility that I could go to college and get out of the town I was in. And it really had to be a dream, because I was involved in an event that I never should have been in. I mean I was involved in throwing the javelin, and I was 125 pounds when I was a senior in high school, so I didn't have the physical makeup to be a javelin thrower.

But that's part of your dreams and part of the things that you work out in your head. I saw a movie, *Samson and Delilah*, and decided to let my hair grow because I felt that perhaps that was the answer. And the longer my hair got, the stronger I got.

The javelin is a biblical weapon. Did that have an appeal to you?

LANDON: Absolutely. If you recall, they were used in the movie, and I was really into that. I had very long hair when I went to SC—they shaved my head, and I couldn't throw the javelin. Guys held me down and shaved my head because everybody had a crew cut but me. And that was the end of it. I mean, I just couldn't throw anymore.

That sounds like a real trauma.

LANDON: It was! I finally quit school because I was injured. After that I got frustrated, and I kept throwing and throwing and throwing until I injured my arm. Then they tried to make me continue to throw. The pain was so great, and they kept shooting me up three times a week with cortisone and Novocain. And then they would embarrass you, you know, because if you're injured and they figured you may not heal up, they'd just as soon you got out of school because they only have so many scholarships.

So they humiliate you. They call you "chickenshit" because you're not throwing and make you do very demeaning jobs. So I finally quit. But I didn't quit on the basis that I felt very sorry for myself. I quit on the basis that I was going to build myself up. I got a job unloading freight cars because I wanted to get way stronger than I was before and then enroll in UCLA and then just beat the shit out of USC. [*Laughs*] That was my *whole dream.*

Did you go to UCLA after that?

LANDON: No. Because when I had the job unloading freight cars, the guy I worked with had a scene to do at Warner Brothers and wanted a partner. It was a very emotional scene from *Home of the Brave.* In the movie *Home of the Brave,* the lead character in the play was actually a Jew. But they changed it to a black man when they made the movie.

Frank Lovejoy was in that one.

LANDON: Right. *Wonderful* movie! That movie, by the way, was shot in about a week. It was weeks of rehearsal, and then they just went in and banged that thing out, and they did a wonderful job. There was tremendous excitement in that film. Anyway, he didn't want to take the emotional part, and he gave it to me. That was the first time I'd had an emotional part to do. *And I loved it.* When I got into [Warner Brothers' acting] school [in 1956], there was no pay involved, but that really got me started.

What was your acting and writing debut?

LANDON: My acting debut, believe it or not, was in a play called *The Bat* in Haddonfield, New Jersey. I played a Japanese houseboy. It's kind of a gothic mystery. And I didn't go over to read for it. My sister wanted to be an actress. She's three years older than I am, and she wanted to go over there, but she was afraid to go by herself. So I went over there with her and sat there, and she read for one of the parts. She didn't get the part.

At that time, in Haddonfield and Collingswood, a couple of small towns, there was no Oriental population whatsoever. And if there were, they weren't looking to be in a play or anything. I was the only young guy sitting out there. So they said, "Do you have any interest in reading for this?" So I said, "Sure. I don't care." I mean it didn't make any difference to me.

So I read for it, and I got the part. And that was the first time I'd ever been onstage. It was very exciting for me, because I was fourteen years old. I couldn't let the kids in my high school know about it—thank God it was in Haddonfield, because they would have razzed me to death. But I was fourteen years old and everyone else in the play, they were all adults. So it was big time for me, getting to go out at night and rehearse and all that stuff.

It helped my self-confidence a great deal. I found out that I was not shy when I was somebody else. Otherwise I was a very shy guy. I would hide my shyness by being the class clown and screwing around, but that was just a cover.

I was very excited to be onstage. *Too* excited as it turned out. The opening line in the play is "Jujitsu pretty good stuff." That's when I throw the leading man onto the stage in the beginning from the wings, and I broke his arm over the thing! I was so loaded with adrenaline . . . It was just terrible!

I've heard you affirm in an interview on "Entertainment Tonight" the positive need to overcome the fear of failure—using failure as a strengthening experience. Have you had to overcome great disappointments to achieve success?

LANDON: Well, I think probably like anybody else. If you want to be in this business, you really have to work out a plan for yourself that enables you to survive with a good healthy ego intact. I mean being told no, no, no, interview after interview, when you don't get the parts—that's very tough for a lot of people. A lot of people have a difficult time handling that because you begin to think those people are right who didn't hire you, and early on I just took the attitude that if they didn't hire me, they had no taste!

That's a fighter's attitude!

LANDON: Absolutely! My attitude was "What a stupid mistake!" The guy they hired was nowhere near as good as I am. But then, to ensure that I would get more jobs, I did all my own stunts. So I would immediately tell a guy when I went in for a television show that had a big fight scene in it, "By the way, I do all my own fights." Because I used to double other actors doing fights.

Well, when you're working for scale, the stuntman's making the same money you are. So instead of paying me ninety dollars and another guy ninety dollars for a day's work, they could get me for the ninety bucks and save the other ninety. So I'd end up getting more jobs that way.

~

MICHAEL WOULD SOMETIMES RECALL HOW DURING THOSE lean years as a struggling actor he had often resorted to active measures to get a shot at a part. Before he obtained his SAG (Screen Actors Guild) card, he would wait in parking lots to corner a casting director for a chance to audition. He could take either the active or the passive tack toward building a career, and in Hollywood the passive tack generally led to obscurity, even starvation.

It was his audacity and downright pugnaciousness that often brought Landon those hard-won career opportunities in a fickle and competitive industry. Over the years, as he pushed for the opportunity to write, direct, and, ultimately, produce, the stakes got higher, and as he wrangled with network executives for the power to control his creative destiny as an independent producer, his methods were refined into those of a diplomat among warriors. But it was the crucible of those difficult early years that forged his tenacity. The scrapper's instinct that had years before won him those ninety-dollar jobs never left him.

"Michael had an enduring youthfulness as well, but what I admire about him was that he was able to go on and create and direct and write these marvelous movies for television."

DOUG MCCLURE

5

NEW DIRECTIONS

"I WAS LUCKY ENOUGH TO BE WORKING IN AN AGE WHEN I thought television was just extraordinary," Michael Landon said of the time when he entered the industry. "The people you did the work for really cared about the work when you were finished. It wasn't just how much the work cost and what rating you got for the work."

Landon's early acting credits included roles in many episodes of such high-quality programs as "Playhouse 90" and "Studio One." His work in a West Coast stage production of *Tea and Sympathy* was well reviewed, and he gave an impressively sensitive performance in the TV special "Telephone Time: The Mystery of Caspar Hauser." Michael had a starring role in his feature film, the 1957 horror flick *I Was a Teen-age Werewolf*, now a cult classic.

In 1957 Michael appeared in an episode of a western series called "The Restless Gun," and producer David Dortort was singularly impressed by the youngster's performance. A new idea for yet another TV western was simmering in Dortort's mind, and when "Bonanza" was conceived two years later, Michael was assigned the coveted role of Little Joe Cartwright. It was on that series that Landon, after years of intense study of both his own craft and television production, chose to make his writing and directing debut.

While Michael's star rose at Paramount Studio, another young actor named Doug McClure had embarked on his own promising career, starring as Trampas in the long-running western series "The Virginian" at Universal Studio. The two men formed a friendship that, despite the different courses their respective careers followed, was to last throughout Michael's life. "Doug," Michael once remarked to me shortly after a reunion with McClure, "has always been one of the really nice people in the business. He was always like a kid."

The remark, I think, is characteristic of Michael's instinctual paternal perceptiveness. I spent time with both guys, and it was easy to see the bond of enduring boyishness between them. But the kid in Michael was streetwise, tough, and boisterous, while the juvenile in Doug (whom I count as a close friend) is something like that of the perennial wide-eyed sophomore. That's not to say that Doug isn't savvy, but the two men were a contrast, both physically and temperamentally.

Little Joe and lanky Trampas could have been a kind of Butch and Sundance duo had they ever been cast as partners in the same western. At fifty-seven, McClure's blond surfer good looks have weathered into a countenance of defined maturity tempered by an easygoing and thoughtful gentle nature.

Michael was as compellingly intense as Doug is consistently affable. Yet there were also strong similarities that bound them together as friends, especially during their years as ambitious young leading men, which Doug recalled fondly one afternoon at his home.

Doug McClure: I first met Michael early in his career while we were both very young actors sharing dreams. I was doing my first series, which was called "Overland Trail," and shortly after got my real break in "The Virginian" at about the same time that Michael landed his role on "Bonanza." I remember going over to his house while he was married to his first wife, Dodie, and finding it full of snakes and little animals and other things especially there for kids.

I would take my daughter Tané to rodeos and fairs, and since Michael and I were both cowboy stars, a lot of kids would rush to us at these events. Michael seemed to love it. He would actually act out scenes with them, playing as if they were all cowboys and he was going to shoot them. The kids would really get into it and act out death scenes, and Michael would giggle and laugh at their drama. He would spend hours in the hotel swimming pool playing water polo and other games with the children and finally come out looking like a *prune*. Even in those days, I could see and admire this warm father quality within him that I think really came out years later in "Little House on the Prairie."

This is only an assumption, but I believe that as kids growing up we had very similar dreams in wanting to live out adventures as heroes. A lot of these feelings came from movies, especially westerns. I know that Mike's father was a projectionist in a movie house. As a kid I used to go to the Bay Theater in Pacific Palisades and dream of one day doing a movie with one of my heroes, like Burt Lancaster. That dream later came true when Burt and I worked together in *The Unforgiven*.

The spirit of my friendship with Michael during those early years, I think, was the living of our dreams. I suppose, being on "Bonanza" and "The Virginian" and being young, it was like saying "You're on the Redskins team and I'm on the Rams team." So there was a sense of friendly competition in the way that we were trying to do the best we could being Little Joe or Trampas.

You mentioned that Michael had referred to me as a kind of "little boy." I think we both had that in common. Michael had an enduring youthfulness as well, but what I admire about him was that he was able to go on and create and direct and write these marvelous movies for television. That was something that I had wanted to do at that time as well, but the "little boy" in me, who was willing to please people by just being the actor, interfered. Michael never let it get in his way.

~

When did you first direct?

LANDON: My first directing job was on "Bonanza," and I'd wanted to direct for a long time. But there was an attitude about me from David Dortort, who was the executive producer. I had written several episodes by that time, but because I was "Little Joe Cartwright"—I mean even the crew felt the same way, that I was just this wild kid.

We were on a riverboat in Lake Tahoe with two hundred members of the press, and David was making another one of his long-winded speeches. When he came to introducing me, he said, "And here is a young actor, a fine actor who's written some screenplays, and—who knows—someday he may even direct."

Well, I jumped up! I was sitting in the front, and I jumped up and said, "When?" I said, "I mean you've got two hundred members of the press here—*when*?" Well, now all these guys are behind me. They start cheering, and Dortort says, "Well, uh, I'll go back, when we get back to L.A., I'll, uh, check the schedule and see if we have an opening."

I said, "Show seventeen! Nobody's set for show seventeen!" I said, "I've already got the screenplay written!" So he said, "Well, uh . . ." I had him! I mean he was dead! He was in front of two hundred members of the press! He said, "All right! Show seventeen!" So everyone started cheering. That's how I got the first job.

~

A lot in this industry has been said about the tremendous loyalty that your production family has for you. Did this paternal closeness begin with "Little House"?

LANDON: Well, some of it with "Bonanza." You know, a lot of guys that were with me on "Bonanza" are still with me. My cinematographer on this film that we're doing now [*Where Pigeons Go to Die*] is [Haskell] Buzz Boggs, and this will be the thirtieth year that Buzz and I have worked together—almost—and exclusively really, aside from a few alternating directors.

How long have you all been together?

LANDON: You mean the whole group? You see, some people have changed. Some have retired, some have passed away. But overall—it's been mostly guys—at least sixteen, seventeen . . .

~

THE CREW ON "BONANZA" BECAME THE NUCLEUS OF Landon's own production family. It was on "Bonanza" that he met and eventually formed a partnership with Kent McCray, who worked as the show's production manager. Despite a stormy beginning, their friendship and professional alliance were to last throughout Landon's life.

Michael openly cherished those salad years with "Bonanza." In our casual conversations he often referred to some hilarious event or stunt that either he or Dan Blocker had pulled. He obviously had a great affection for both Blocker and Lorne Greene. Michael was a born mimic, and he reveled in his ponderous imitation of Greene's lordly bearing and baritone voice.

On one occasion he gleefully told me of a scene they were shooting on what once was the frontier street for Virginia City. "Lorne," Michael explained, "was particularly proud of the fact that he had all of his own teeth in perfect condition, or so he claimed." Between takes, Landon noticed the actor furtively searching for something on the dirt street.

"What are you looking for?" asked Michael curiously. Greene "ahemed" and answered guardedly, "Oh, I lost a contact lens." Michael gazed at him full in the face and replied, "Well, it looks like you lost both of them."

Sensing that something wasn't on the up-and-up, Michael began searching the ground. At length he found a large false tooth with a spike on one end. Picking it up as he walked up to Greene, he said innocently, "Oh, by the way, Lorne, I found your contact lens."

Startled, Greene asked, "Where is it?" Suddenly Michael's face broke into a mischievous grin as he held up the spiked tooth as if to insert it in the silver-haired actor's eye. "Here it is!" he announced.

"Bonanza" crew members have told me of the almost brotherly relationship that Michael had with Dan Blocker. Greatly saddened when Blocker died in 1972, Landon wrote and directed a special tribute episode to his friend titled "Forever." It was a beautiful and sensitive paean to Blocker that also revealed Landon's growing power and scope as a writer and director.

"Bonanza" served Michael as a training ground in television production. He had done his apprenticeship behind the camera and in the studio cutting rooms, intently studying every aspect of cinematography and film editing.

When the sets for the show were finally struck, Landon was ready to move on. He nurtured another ambition now—to produce his own property—and was alert to new projects.

Having gained popularity as a young star, and with impressive writing and directing credits to his name, he was a hot property. Shortly after "Bonanza" closed, producer Ed Friendly approached Landon with the rights to a series of children's books by Laura Ingalls Wilder that he had purchased for three thousand dollars. Friendly proposed that they coproduce and that Michael star in a series based on the books. Landon stipulated that he would undertake the venture on the condition that he be the sole producer of the show. The two men would split the profits. Friendly agreed, and Michael reunited much of the old "Bonanza" crew and commenced work as the executive producer of the new series "Little House on the Prairie."

~

How was "Little House on the Prairie" conceived?

LANDON: Well, first Ed Friendly came to me and had the screenplay and the books. I took the books home and gave one of the books to my daughter and had her read them. I read the screenplay. I thought it could be a very, very good show for the whole family to sit down and watch without it being a "kiddie-kid show," you know? And it just turned out very well. The cast was wonderful in the show; we had some really good people.

~

DURING THE FIRST SEASON OF PRODUCTION ON "LITTLE House," a conflict developed between Landon and Ed Friendly regarding creative control of the show. The discord led to Friendly's leaving the show, although his name as co-executive producer continued to be aired on the credits. As a virtual figurehead producer, he retained his contractual share of the series' profits, which eventually earned both him and Landon a fortune.

~

On "Little House on the Prairie" you were executive producer, but it said "Ed Friendly" at the end . . .

LANDON: Ed was never there. He never came to the set. He never had anything to do with the show. Ed was very angry with me in the beginning, and *TV Guide* again jumped all over me, as they seemed to love to do, without ever finding out—no one ever interviews me. I've had problems with only a couple of people in my life. Ed Friendly was one.

I must be very honest with you that the only reason I

had trouble with these people is because they do not know what they're doing. And all they're concerned about is their egos—and having interviews. And that isn't what this business is about.

Talking about yourself isn't the real exciting part. I mean it is for these kinds of people because that's all they really can do. But that was my major problem with these two people. . . . It was as though I had somehow offended these people when in fact you could ask any member of the crews on either one of these productions, and you'd find out that the backing was for me a hundred percent, because everyone wants to do a good job and get the best product they can. I mean, it's no fun busting your tail for someone who doesn't know what they're doing. And in both cases that was the problem.

Ed did his best to sabotage the show, and fortunately he didn't, because he made about forty million dollars from it.

~

DESPITE THE RIFT WITH FRIENDLY, THE SHOW BECAME immensely popular. Landon portrayed the young farmer Charles Ingalls as a sensitive, plainspoken, and proud man of grass-roots integrity and open emotions. It was an impressive departure from the roguish Little Joe role of his previous series, and a great deal of the poignant quality in "Little House on the Prairie" issues from the complexity that Landon was able to bring to the character. Other principals in the cast included Karen Grassle as Charles's wife, Caroline; Melissa Gilbert as Laura Ingalls; and Melissa Sue Anderson as Laura's older sister, Mary. Together they formed the core of an ensemble cast of extraordinary appeal.

Termed by reviewers as "wholesome family entertainment," "LHOTP" won a vast and loyal audience that was drawn to the nostalgic sentimentality of the show. It was this very quality of traditional romanticism that also caused numerous critics to label the show "sappy" or maudlin. Never mind the reviewers' barbs. The people loved "Little House on the Prairie."

As producer, writer, director, and star, Landon crafted, coordinated, and controlled virtually every aspect of the show's production. His personal capacity for impassioned work was staggering, and all of this focused creative intensity, complemented by Kent McCray's managerial genius, engineered one of the most efficient and harmonious production companies in Hollywood.

"Michael and Kent worked extremely well together," recalls Harry Flynn. "The operation in general always seemed to go smoothly, although there are always problems that come up. In general the cast and crew were extremely happy, and they were extremely loyal to Michael."

Actress Pamela Roylance, who joined the show for its final season in the role of Sarah Carter, recalled in 1989 how the opportunity to work with Michael Landon was for her the fulfillment of a personal dream.

PAMELA ROYLANCE: I was born in Seattle but raised in Portland, Oregon, all of my life, and I taught high school up there for about three years. I had studied theater and wanted to spend my life as an actress. Finally, in 1980, I took a year's leave of absence from teaching and moved down to L.A. The door was still open to go back to teaching, but after sticking it out with some very difficult times for about a year I began to get auditions, which led to receiving the role on "Little House."

I had gone in for an audition quite early because Michael went out of town. They were kind of screening people before he came back. When he finally got back into town a couple of months later, I was able to see him. I was pretty green when he met me. I had no experience, and he hired me from nowhere. Even during the auditions he made me feel so good because he gave me immediate response. After it was over he said, "Terrific!" His arm went up in the air, and he said, "Terrific!"

And I thought, Gee, no one's done that before. He must really mean what he says. And then when he had me back a second time, he did it again, and I thought, I know I'm on the money. It was wonderful to have him believe in me when I had no credits. I love that he does that. He gives people opportunity. He sees something there, and then he gives you the opportunity. He gives you the chance.

When I still taught school, I would go home and, while I was making dinner, turn on the television and watch "Little House" all the time. I used to think to myself, I want to go to L.A. and either do Walt Disney stuff or "Eight Is Enough" or "Little House on the Prairie." Those were the dreams.

I'll never forget the first time I walked on the set. We were doing the inside shoot at MGM, and just to see that whole complete house inside that giant studio really surprises you. It was very touching. The moment it got me was when we'd gone inside and it was all lit and all ready for us, so we were just working our marks out.

We were standing there for just a moment being situated and getting ready, and I looked upstairs at that loft and thought to myself, I cannot believe that I, Pamela Roylance, am standing here in this Little House that I used to watch on TV and look up and see those two little girls up there, and now I'm going to look up and see those two little boys who will play my sons. This is something I really love and believe in, because I *love* that kind of television. It was my opportunity to be the person in all the world that got to do it. It was overwhelming and touching. All I could feel was this incredible gratitude and good fortune.

I remember one time when we were on the set and I had a question to ask him during a break. There was so much activity going on, a lot of noise and everything, but he gave me his full attention and his eyes were focused right on my eyes and he just looked right at me, his attention and his eye contact never wavering. He waited until I was completely done asking my question, letting me explain everything and get the whole question out. When he answered it, he took his time and he was right there with exactly what I needed for the answer. I thought he had finished talking, so I had begun to speak again when he started talking too, and then he stopped. I had interrupted him, not meaning to, but he stopped and let me go on. But everything was going on, and he was giving me all of this undivided attention. And I watched him do it constantly, with other people, especially with the children on the set. He was right there for you.

"LITTLE HOUSE ON THE PRAIRIE" CONTINUED THROUGH the 1983 and 1984 seasons, and the show went out with a bang. Michael had persuaded network executives to let him wind up the series with three television movies.

When the sets for the farmhouses and the town of Walnut Grove had originally been built, Michael had painstakingly researched their historical accuracy. The various false fronts, facades of what became to viewers such familiar buildings as Oleson's Mercantile, the schoolhouse, and the church, had over the years become like a second home to the cast and crew. The lease on the land in Simi Valley where all of this had been built stipulated that the property be returned in the same condition in which it had been found.

The thought of those beloved structures being bulldozed was painful to Landon. Instead he scripted a story that allowed the townfolk, in an act of defiance, to blow up their own homes and businesses rather than let an avaricious railroad company occupy them. The buildings were blasted apart in a series of spectacular explosions filmed for that final show, titled *Little House: The Last Farewell*, in 1984. When it was all over, the beloved television town had returned to the mustard grass from which it had risen nine years earlier.

There is an interesting postscript to this story. A day or so after the sets had been demolished, Maury Dexter, who had for years worked as an assistant director on many of Landon's series shows, drove out to the area in a pickup truck and salvaged enough lumber to construct a deck for his home. I find it somewhat comforting to know that the town of Walnut Grove lives on as part of the exterior of Maury's house.

"Oh, I got excited to see my name on the trucks! I must admit: little kid from Jersey got his name on the trucks—I mean that was big stuff!"
MICHAEL LANDON

6

MICHAEL LANDON PRODUCTIONS

MICHAEL LANDON'S THIRD TELEVISION SERIES, "HIGHWAY to Heaven," had been something of a tough sell. Right on the heels of the "LHOTP" swan song, Landon set to work to present the NBC executives with his concept. Because of the conspicuous success of his last series, he had the clout to get a respectful hearing from NBC as an independent producer.

Even so, the story premise he suggested for the prospective new property met with something of a stone wall of skepticism. Landon proposed to do a show about a probationary angel sent to Earth on a series of heavenly assignments to aid mortals with very human problems. Unlike his two previous series, this one called for no large supporting cast, no resident family, and no home base hearth. The only other regular on the show would be a cynical, hardboiled former cop as the unlikely ally of this angel, sharing with him the vagabond existence of divine missions.

Despite considerable misgivings, the network agreed to a pilot for the show. The feature, starring Landon as the angel, Jonathan Smith, and "LHOTP" veteran Victor French as his buddy, Mark Gordon, first aired in 1984. The ratings were encouraging enough for the show to be picked up as a series.

With but few exceptions Michael directed virtually every episode of "Highway to Heaven" as well as writing many. The series' five-year run from 1984 to 1989 brought him to the height of his creative power, and the show's flexible premise allowed him to address forthrightly many of the political, social, and environmental issues to which he was strongly committed—issues such as water conservation, suburban racial integration, the rights of disabled people, and the advancement of cancer research.

The series drew both praise and censure from critics. Landon's angelic character was derided by some reviewers as being sanctimonious, and the show was dismissed as being preachy and self-righteous. Michael was never a fence sitter, and he nurtured an almost missionary sense of purpose in his work. Much of the entertainment he produced made definite moralistic statements. These messages, I believe, were often calculated simply to draw viewers into a stronger personal involvement with the larger issues of humanity.

"Highway to Heaven" became a significant summit in Michael's career because the show was the first vehicle to be produced under the banner of his own production company, Michael Landon Productions.

~

Was it a struggle to get the series "Highway to Heaven" sold?

LANDON: Oh, yeah! When I had the meeting with them, they knew I was gonna talk to them about a series idea. And they had actually suggested several ideas to me. Basically detectives was what they all wanted. So, when I went into this meeting—I guess there were probably six or seven guys—I told them that what I wanted to do was this series where I'm an angel. There was just a great big silence. I mean [*begins to laugh*] I kept looking at everybody, right? They were all attempting not to meet my eyes! You know, because actually their eyes were rolled up in their heads!

The whole notion of that horrified them! They said, "Well, you know those things don't do well."

And I said, "Because no one's really gone ahead and done it. They've done it as though the angel was a joke, but no one's ever done it believing it. You have to believe it if you're gonna do it."

So, I took the pressure off them anyway. I said, "Look. I'll do this pilot, and then I'll do another pilot. I mean, if this pilot doesn't do well, if it doesn't test well, then I'll do another pilot for you. You're not going to lose anything. You'll just have a two-hour movie." So on that basis it was fine.

I silently applauded to myself when "Highway to Heaven" came on the air, and I watched the first episode, and at the very end it said "a Michael Landon Production," which it never said as far as I know on "Little House on the Prairie" . . .

LANDON: Right.

I just got this feeling that you decided, Forget it, I'm just gonna do it my way, I'm gonna have my production company . . .

LANDON: Actually "Little House" I did my own way. I didn't have anybody telling me what to do on that show either. I'll give NBC a lot of credit there. They were never on my back—never demanded anything, never made any waves at all. They were wonderful to work with on "Little House."

The basic difference for using just my own production company for the other show was that I felt that our group could make a show so efficiently that I wouldn't have to worry about deficit financing. I mean, I don't want to take my own money and go in a hole. I love the business, but I don't want to lose money. We were able to be under budget all those years on "Little House," and I felt that we could do the same thing with "Highway," and we did.

And in so doing we were able to share the profits with the crew—you know, money under, we had nice bonuses every year—and it was a better business deal for me because I was then able to syndicate my own product instead of having twenty percent or fifty percent. That was just a business decision.

But it was just such a neat thing to see . . .

LANDON: [*Laughing*] Oh, yeah! Oh, I got excited to see my name on the trucks! I must admit: little kid from Jersey got his name on the trucks—I mean that was big stuff!

I'd appreciate it very much if you would give me your own personal definition of success and fulfillment, if you have one.

LANDON: To be honest with you, I think it's knowing what you're doing and enjoying it and having the people around you enjoy it too—having a company where everybody comes to work early because they know it's so much fun to be there. And believe it or not, that's what we have here.

~

I understand that the idea of "Highway to Heaven" was conceived in a traffic jam. Is that true?

LANDON: Yeah. I was driving through Beverly Hills, and everybody was cursing at each other and honking their horns. You're bumper to bumper. You can't go anywhere, and I thought to myself, All this energy! I mean, if they would just take a little bit of this energy and use it to be nice to each other, traffic would flow like it generally does in Europe, where people have learned to get along—not to try to cut you out but calmly let you in. I mean, you don't see any of that stuff generally when you're driving in Europe! Everybody really helps each other. If they didn't, you'd be in deep trouble! You haven't got any lights worth a damn over there! Everything is cir—can you imagine having circles in L.A., where people all blend into a circle? Can you imagine what that would be like? Why, it would be a *war!*

And the reason I made the guy an angel, which I know NBC didn't like, was because I think people have such a low opinion of human beings that they would say, "I don't believe this guy. I mean this guy's not gonna go around doing this kind of stuff." Plus, it also gave me the freedom to be anybody I wanted to be. I could be a doctor, I could be a lawyer, I could be this, I could be that, because I was an angel! I could come up with all of the information, all the papers, anything I needed. So it just made an easy vehicle for us to move around and get involved in a lot of different situations.

You know the opening sequence of that has you walking on a road. It reminds me a lot of Henry Fonda in The Grapes of Wrath. *I was wondering, was that classic sort of an inspiration?*

LANDON: No.

This was something you just conceived on your own, and out it came.

LANDON: [*Softly*] Yeah.

~

MICHAEL LANDON PRODUCTIONS

RIGHT ON THE HEELS OF OUR FIRST CONVERSATION, MI-
chael revealed a facet of his nature that I was to see as a
consistent, endearing trait. Very often, when work was
over (although he still had a day of editing ahead), Michael
enjoyed having some of his people stick around if they
could, just to unwind. I now see that as part of the boy in
Michael coming out. He was like the shyly affectionate kid
who liked to hang out with a buddy or two at the play-
ground after school and share with them whatever was
earnestly cherished or mischievously, hilariously appre-
ciated.

As Harry and I turned to go, we heard Michael's voice
call us back. "Would you guys like to see a bird being
born?" he asked from behind the moviola with his film
editor, Jerry Taylor. We reentered the room as the monitor
began its chatter once again. Taylor was running the
rushes of the made-for-TV movie *Where Pigeons Go to Die*,
Michael's major project at the time, and we had been invited to stay awhile and watch.

As Taylor rewound the film, Michael set up the clip
we would see by explaining that the film opens with the
hatching of a bird. "The pigeon," joked Michael, "eventually gets into a cross-country race for home when he gets,
among other things, attacked by a hawk, chased by a cat,
and shot with a BB gun. Oh, he really has a tough week!"

We stood beside Michael and stared into the little
flickering screen as the first sequence for the film depicted
the gradual, triumphant emergence of a tiny baby pigeon
from its shell. The exultant intimacy of that scene merged

into a tapestry of other shots that climaxed in the bold flight of a white fledgling against a blue autumn sky.

"We shot that pigeon in front of a Ritter [fan]," Michael explained with unmasked professional pride. "That's the first time a pigeon has been filmed in this manner. It's done all the time with soaring birds, but never with a flyer like a pigeon."

A panoramic shot of a high bridge dwarfed by a broad, placid river followed. "And now we go to title," Michael remarked in a soft voice as if he had spoken only to himself as he watched intently.

So the odyssey began, the first footage of what proved to be a marvelous motion picture. It was, however, the flickering images of that virgin film footage that remained printed on my mind. Moment to moment, they were literally the realization of an artist's vision and of his dream. I was glad to have been given a glimpse of what he had seen.

"I think an awful lot of people destroy their lives by spending their lives with expectations instead of just living within the moment and enjoying the dream."
                                        MICHAEL LANDON

7

ON DREAMS AND LIVING

THE COUNSEL OF THE LATE EDUCATOR AND AUTHOR JO-seph Campbell, to follow our bliss, would have found great validation, I believe, in the personal mythology of Michael Landon. Michael followed his bliss by living his dreams. Introspective by nature, he was ever alert and responsive to the creative instinct within him to experience and express his inner vision.

Our first conversation had left me with a strong impression of his questing drive, and it was to provide the theme for *Yesteryears'* Michael Landon Productions issue. The edition went to press in late fall 1989, a few weeks after my introduction to him at Lorimar Studio. Researching and composing the necessary material turned out to be great fun personally, for it was to lead to an association with several individuals who had worked with Michael on various properties.

By and large, they were a gracious and cooperative group, and many of those people have since become close friends. The energy and communication I received from these folks was a validation of Landon's own assertion of the family spirit that they all shared. One of the most enlightening encounters was with Brianne Murphy, whom I had actually met a few weeks before my introduction to Michael.

For several years Brianne worked as a director of photography for Michael, as part of a triumvirate of cinematographers that also included Haskell (Buzz) Boggs and Ted Voigtlander. She carries the singular distinction of being the first and, I believe, still only woman cinematographer in the American film industry.

Brianne is a remarkable artist in her own right. In an industry and community like Hollywood, where the attitude about employing women in key positions in production is in many ways atrociously prejudiced, Brianne has tenaciously fought for a career that has borne fruit both creatively and with such glittering laurels as an Oscar and an Emmy.

Alongside the publication of our entertainment quarterly, I had begun work on a book profiling certain celebrities I had interviewed during the past two years. The proposed theme of the book would hopefully provide these people with a forum for discussing their personal concepts of success and happiness. Brianne had been one of the artists I had included in the volume, and I had hoped that Michael (who I had been told by Harry Flynn simply did not do books) could be persuaded to contribute.

Brianne had encouraged me to press the matter. She had run into her old boss one day in a hallway outside the cutting room where Michael was working. "Mike took to you," she told me later. "I think he'd consider it."

I sent a few copies of our quarterly out to Michael's office, and he was apparently pleased with the results. The issue resembled a large family album, which, as it turned out, was probably entirely appropriate to the spirit of his production clan.

At about this time I had somehow worked up a hunch that Michael might agree to work on a book elaborating the personal and professional philosophy he had begun to address in our first conversation. Harry agreed to ask him, and I began preparing questions for an anticipated meeting based on similar past interviews, when I had structured the questions to guide the subject through a development of philosophical themes.

After spending a few days working on these notes, I concluded that such a structure would probably be gratuitous with Landon. Throughout our first conversation I had sensed in the man an intuitive perceptiveness that could alone lead to profound revelations. Shuffling through the scrawled pages of a yellow legal pad, I culled the list to about one-third of its previous length and decided to wing it.

While Landon had a reputation among reporters for

being dominating, wary, and generally a difficult interview, that had not been my initial impression of the man at all. I had sensed rather an open intelligence and an intuitive sense of creative communication. I discussed my thoughts about the second conversation with Brianne Murphy, who agreed with the approach I planned to take. "He'll know where you're coming from," she affirmed. "And he'll know where you're headed." As one of Landon's cinematographers, Brianne was in a prime position to experience the man's way of controlled spontaneity and those times of relinquishment when he simply "lived the dream."

BRIANNE MURPHY: When Michael did a script, he was reading it like he hadn't seen it before when you know that he had written it. He would look at it, and then he'd stay at his table and close his eyes, and I guess what he was doing was visualizing that scene edited. And once he'd done that—and nobody bothered him while he did it—he would come to me and say, "This is the shot."

He knew from there to the next one to the next one just where it was going. And he very seldom went from the beginning of the scene to the end of the scene. He'd cut and change angles and cover, because he knew exactly where he was going to put the scissors. Sometimes actors would be all fired up and ready to do the entire scene, and he'd say, "OK, cut! All right, now we're over here, Bri." And the actors: "But, but . . ." They quickly gained confidence in him. They might as well, because he wasn't going to change it. He knew what he was doing. He always knew what he was doing.

I received a response to my request more quickly than expected. In an answering machine message that greeted me one evening, Harry suggested I interview Michael for the proposed book the following week at the Malibu office he had leased since winding up the production of "Highway to Heaven." Our meeting was set for a Thursday at 3:00 P.M., because earlier that day Michael would be appearing in a downtown courtroom to make a public statement regarding his stand on possible reforms in foster-home programs.

That day I drove to Harry's house in the valley, and he sensibly offered to drive since I hadn't the vaguest notion of where we were going. About thirty minutes later we pulled off Pacific Coast Highway up along a demure driveway to a small parking lot behind a pleasant-looking midsize modern office building with ample windows. The setting was nearly pastoral, with the ocean across the road facing the front of the building and a hillside covered with lavender ice plant sloping up toward the Santa Monica Mountains in the rear.

Harry led the way to the front office and introduced me to Evy Wagner, Michael's secretary. We could hear boisterous voices in the next room, and we stepped through the short hall to see Michael sitting at a card game with Kent McCray, where the two were good-naturedly swearing at each other over a couple of cans of light beer. The place was full of snacks. Harry introduced me to Kent and foraged for some garlic bagel chips. Michael looked up from his chair, grinning, and shook my hand. "How have ya been?" he asked with real warmth.

While the partners finished playing their hand, Harry chatted with them about various friends and family members. I felt encouraged to join in the banter a little and sensed no resistance to this. Kent is an immensely likable guy, boisterous, down to earth, and bluntly honest. His wife, Susan, whom I was to meet later, worked as Landon's casting director and was the third member of a siblinglike trio that formed the core of Michael's production family.

Michael tossed his cards on the table and got to his feet. "Well, I guess it's about time we got to work," he said cheerfully. The comment pleased me greatly, since I had relished the prospect of doing such work with Landon ever since that evening on Main Street back in 1986. He then led the way to a side office furnished with two sofas forming a right angle with a coffee table before them. Michael and I sat on the corners facing each other while I placed the tiny recorder on the table. "So, how have ya been?" he repeated with an open smile. The man seemed genuinely pleased to see me, and I was moved.

I explained the premise of the book, which was (and, at press time, still is) being composed under the working title *Personal Summits.* "My perception of you," I ventured to him, "would be as the individual who synopsizes the entire spirit of this thing." I told him about how I had trimmed down the usual structure of questions and how convinced I was that whatever he chose to share would be dynamic if I just let him have his head.

I was surprised at how easily I had overcome my diffidence. Michael had listened intently to all of this, and despite the fact that mine was the role of interviewer, I could not help sensing the kind of incisive energy that he, as a director, imparted to his actors.

~

In our last conversation you remarked that you believed in dreams but not in expectations. How do you distinguish between the two?

LANDON: Dreams don't give you disappointments. You're never disappointed when you dream, because you're not expecting anything. Expectations mean you must reach whatever that dream might have been. I think an awful lot of people destroy their lives by spending their lives with expectations instead of just living within the moment and enjoying the dream.

Even if you *reach* the expectation, the fact that you had it, the expectation, means that it won't mean much. Because in essence you *expected* it to happen. So, it's not wondrous, it's not joyous, it's as it was supposed to be. And always disappointing.

More so expectations involving other people. I think it's one of the things that wrecks a lot of relationships. Marry the person, but don't have expectations for what that person's gonna become or do—just love what you've got. And don't have expectations of what it's going to become, because it can only be disappointing.

It seems like an enforced limitation on a broader concept of faith. If you have faith in a dream, the dream has a divinity of its own.

LANDON: Absolutely! It's all you need! Enjoy, enjoy it.

How many careers do you see, not just in my business but in everybody's, where, because of this moment of success, suddenly you have expectations about where this career is going? I mean you've already got part of a dream. Enjoy that. But if you have expectations that this dream is going to continue and build and get larger in the *real* sense of larger, most are gonna be disappointed. *Very* disappointed.

You've described what an expectation is. What is a dream?

LANDON: Oh, a dream is that wonderful private time that the child within all of us can enjoy—can wake up happier because of—can day by day be happier because a small portion of that dream, *without expectations*, can happen in any day of your life.

I think, for instance, everybody dreams that you can

change someone else's life for the better. I don't think changing your own life for the better, whether it be financially or anything else, is quite as important. It doesn't mean quite as much as when suddenly you see that someone else's life is better and you know you've affected them.

When I was a kid, I wanted to be a doctor because my dream was seeing this smiling child come into my office after I had saved the child's life. If as a doctor I had expectations of saving the lives of *all* the children I see, my life would be a torment—and life *is* torment for many doctors. You *know* that an awful lot of doctors are involved in drugs, and I don't think it's because of the availability of drugs; I think it's because they've had too many expectations for their patients.

You've been a dreamer all your life, I would assume. I feel that.

LANDON: I spent my whole childhood dreaming. Alone! It was my escape. I dug a hole up in a hill and dreamed!

Well, what are the dreams that you cherish now?

LANDON: Well, you know, they alter all the time. My dreams now, because of my younger children and my grandchildren, are dreams of this clean world that's at our fingertips, that we could have if it wasn't for greed and laziness! Did you see the paper and look at the trash? It was like—you couldn't believe it! I mean, here are all of the people coming out for Earth Day, and they leave all of the garbage and all of the slop and everything else. You know, you just hope it doesn't turn into an event, a media event.

CONVERSATIONS WITH MICHAEL LANDON

*And all the time you're saying that you want to save the environ-
ment, but you're sipping your coffee out of a Styrofoam cup.*

LANDON: Right! You gotta start somewhere, I suppose.
But sadly enough, the majority of people, if it affects their
life in any uncomfortable way . . . and in the United States
we find almost *everything* uncomfortable. Getting off our
ass to do anything is uncomfortable because we're so
spoiled.

*It seems your dreams have become so cosmic now simply because
you've already achieved so much on a personal level.*

LANDON: [*Reflects for a moment and laughs*] Either that or
I'm trying to escape from that area because I'm not so sure
that I've accomplished anything. [*Pauses*] Yeah. I'm still
with that one. [*A long pause*]
     You know, if you work all the time, you tend to miss
all of the areas that you go to where your work has really
affected people positively. And you get into a business
syndrome that only has to do with whether your show is
on or off, not whether or not it's really—it's really done
something. Either that or reviewers have gotten to me. I'm
not sure. [*Laughs*]

*I believe in a way you've sort of been ahead of your time. You see,
historically, our own country always seems to have headed
toward great revolutionary changes toward the closing of one
century and into the other. Well, "Little House" and "Highway"
and the work that you did during those two decades really, I think,
were two products that preceded the next renaissance to come.*

You had the creative courage and ability and talent to put together beautiful pieces of entertainment, wonderfully written. They touched so many different people because the themes you touched upon weren't just current topics. They were all wrapped around the nucleus of human understanding: the longing that everybody had for having their own dreams come true, for having a good life, for having a world in which people cared about each other. Those are the themes that mark any great renaissance, whether they are expressed in art or literature or music, and people responded to that.

Not everyone could go to the Louvre or the Metropolitan Museum of Art and see these things. But everyone can turn on the television and see the vividness of your art. So, I've always thought that that was the kind of creative effectiveness that should be emulated.

LANDON: Well, I'd like to play this tape every Monday morning when I come in to work. [*Laughter from both of us*] No, I'm not kidding you! Because you know I am as insecure as any other artist.

We need juicing up, I guess.

~

MICHAEL LANDON EXHIBITED AN EMOTIONAL DICHOTomy that I believe was his instinctive response to two opposing forces within him: idealism and awareness of life's tremendous ironies. It was a divergence that he continually strove to reconcile into a meaningful personal balance. Much of the man's complexity, in fact, is revealed in the nature of paradox. He was a fascinating individual who defied generalization.

He could project tremendous self-confidence and yet occasionally confess to great self-doubt. He was gregarious and reticent, intensely aggressive, yet capable of revealing a poignant gentleness and almost shy affection. He was one of the most competent and professionally focused individuals I have ever met, but he was capable of unbridled hilarity and sheer adolescent rambunctiousness.

He could be adamant in his advancement of certain pragmatic convictions regarding business or politics and yet astonish an intimate the next moment with a touchingly ingenuous expression of an awed faith in divine Providence. There was an absolute genuineness to all of these disparities, for Michael was driven by a relentless motivation to level with others. Above and beyond the vibrant contrasts of his temperament, however, one quality ran constant. He was consistently courageous, one of the most spiritually valiant men I have ever known.

"I'd like to be remembered as someone who was a good guy to work for."

MICHAEL LANDON

8

THE BOSS

ACTORS OFTEN HAVE A TOUGH TIME BEING TAKEN SE-
riously as directors. A performer who aspires to working
behind the camera hazards being winked at as a deluded
upstart with a colossal ego. If he has enough clout as an
actor, he may be indulged, but you can generally cut the
surrounding skepticism regarding his ability with a dull
meat cleaver. Michael Landon proved himself to be one of
the impressive exceptions.

Michael was a man who cherished his reveries. He
was a dreamer all of his life, and his work was the stuff of
which dreams were made. Directing provided him with
the dynamic avenue to give substance to his inner images.

Landon's experience as a performer along with his
tremendous native ability and discipline provided him with
a special insight regarding the motivations of actors. His

considerate treatment of them was consistent with his general work ethic. Because he'd been there, and known the rejection and frustration that is so often the actor's lot, he went to great lengths to exercise patience and understanding regarding the people he employed.

~

In one episode of "Little House" called "The Legacy," I think another one you both wrote and directed, Charles embarks upon an odyssey of self-discovery. What is the legacy that Michael Landon would like to leave to the world?

LANDON: That I was a good guy to work for. That I was fair with people and I never put anybody down. It made no difference what their job was. That was one of the great rules on our set. You know, you get an ensemble cast, you get enough people in a cast, you're gonna get some people who are gonna begin to believe that they are big. Because they're starring in the show. And on our show it made no difference who the star was.

If you verbally abused a crew member, that crew member had the open right in front of everybody to abuse you, because there was *no way* they were going to get fired. And when you have that kind of a situation, you first of all discover that stars who can be a pain in the ass aren't. They're only a pain in the ass when they can get away with being a pain in the ass. But you don't start demeaning people when you know they're gonna nail you. There are so many spoiled people. And their agents don't do them a favor. Their managers don't do them a favor by coddling and catering and doing all these things they do for them—people walking around with six and seven bodyguards—it's a joke. It's all to try and reinforce their importance, and you're never gonna get it that way.

What then would be your personal definition of true wealth and success?

LANDON: Well, for me it's the relationships with the people I work with. The knowledge that we'll all cross that river together. I don't give a damn how tough the water is. That we respect each other on the same level *regardless* of our economic base. That we'll love and care about each other. I mean, you find me any company where everybody cares, and I'm gonna show you a company I'll buy the stock of.

~

FOR A NUMBER OF ACTORS MICHAEL'S FORBEARANCE sometimes preceded even the audition itself. In her autobiography, *As I Am* (Pocket Books/Simon and Schuster, 1988), Patricia Neal fondly recalled receiving a script from Landon for an episode of "Little House on the Prairie" featuring a role she wanted very much to do. Unfortunately, the shooting schedule would disrupt overseas travel plans she had already made with her family. Her agent at that time believed she had lost the part.

Undaunted, Neal called Landon directly to explain her dilemma and was assured by him that she had the part and they would await her return. "Michael is one of the finest directors I have ever worked with," Neal wrote of her subsequent experience. "He understands actors and he understands people."

Robert Caspar, who joined the cast of "Little House on the Prairie" for its final season in the role of Mr. Montague, found himself in a race across town to meet a casting call for the show. As he recalls, that summons led to an introduction to someone who "gave me such a happy time in my life."

ROBERT CASPAR: I got called by my agent to see the casting people. I saw Sue McCray and her assistant, both charming ladies, and that interview seemed to go very successfully. They told me that I would hear from Michael and I would be called in to see him and read for him in a very few days. Time went by, and they canceled that meeting and apologized. This was the time of the great floods, and Michael's house was washing away or something like that. So I said fine, and they'd let me know.

I got the call. One day I was in a bookstore way out in Northridge [a community in the San

Fernando Valley]. I thought I'd call my service, and my agent was raving that I had to be at MGM to see Michael. And I said, "I'm a hundred miles away!" And he said, "Well, you've got to get there."

I raced home, and before I did, I called Sue, and she said I wasn't too late; they would make Michael wait to see me. So I raced home, changed into something very flossy, and raced all the way across town into Culver City. And lo and behold, they had Michael walking the floor. He was pacing! The decision had to be made that day. It was all so sudden. They couldn't give me much of a warning, but there I was.

He must have waited an hour at least, probably an hour and a half. Now, it's much to the credit of Susan and her assistant, who must have liked me extremely much. And what they said to Michael I don't know, but he waited. We talked, I read. Susan read the script with me, and Michael got very near to me and did those funny things with his fingers the way those directors do, looking at my face. Before I read, I said to him, "I hope you listen fast, because I act fast!" Well, he liked that.

After the reading we talked some more. And we talked some more! I was having an absolutely wonderful time. You could see he was pondering and pondering and pondering. We were having this wonderful conversation. I rarely have had such an intensely interesting conversation with a director or producer—or anyone, for that matter, in Hollywood.

I gave him my sympathies about his personal problems out there in Malibu. I remember making the joke that I happened to live on a mountaintop and, thank God, I didn't have that problem. Not long after that, either that evening or the next morning or something like that—it was very shortly—Susan was very kind and called me at home, and she said I had the part. I said to her, "I never enjoyed an interview so much in my life out here in Hollywood. Is he always like that?"

And she said, "Well, he's always very nice, but I never heard him talk like that." She said, "What's more, the part was already cast. The network was insisting to him to cast a certain person that they wanted, that they favored. He said he wasn't having any of that, he was gonna have Bob Caspar." Well, of course, he was my friend for life!

THE BACK-TO-BACK SUCCESS OF HIS OWN TWO TELEVIsion series had kept the people in Landon's production family working for fifteen years. Stories abound of his openhanded generosity in paying the family hospital bills of certain distressed crew members, his magnanimous bonuses and opulent Christmas gifts. Michael had become in effect an institution in television.

He was a phenomenon of professional self-realization in an industry that was in many ways notorious for manipulative suppression of creative sovereignty. As an independent producer he was generally loved and profoundly respected by his own staff, while others beyond the periphery of his professional sphere were often baffled by and envious of the tremendous loyalty of his close-knit ensemble of cast and crew.

Landon's production company impressed me as being a kind of "democratic monarchy." As the boss, he held absolute control over every aspect of his company's artistic and business functions, but it was a subtle control that was tacitly accepted by the cast and crew. Few if any of them, I believe, would have wanted it any other way. At any rate, that was the way it was, and I have never seen a unit of people in the television industry that worked together as effectively or as harmoniously as this team did.

Gene Trindl is a professional photographer who worked consistently with Michael Landon since the actor's first series. A great deal of the drama, hilarity, day-to-day work, and recreational routine, along with some moving glimpses of Michael's home life, has been chronicled through the wonderful images of Gene's photographic artistry. Gene literally lived what he saw and photographed. In reminiscent conversation about Michael one afternoon, he shared some of the thoughts that give voice to his pictures.

GENE TRINDL: I go back to "Bonanza" days with Mike and continued to work with him through "Little House" to "Highway" along with a couple of movies that he's done. I was a freelance photographer for *TV Guide*. On "Bonanza" he was just one of the four guys of a group shot, and he was fine. Just full of hell and cracking jokes, just a nice guy with the rest of them.

Over twenty years I saw some remarkable growth from being just a kid actor to learning how to direct and the whole process of becoming a producer. It was part of my job to photograph him during different times and different stages of his life.

He grew through his experiences through the years like we all do. He was a damn good man and businessman, and actor, producer, director, joke teller. You never worked *for* Mike; you worked *with* Mike. He was still the boss, but he was right there with you, working with you, which I thought was great. He took care of his people.

One of my favorite pictures that I ever took involving Mike that I thought was funny was his press agent, Harry Flynn, getting hit with a pie. We were out there shooting a thing for "Highway to Heaven" where there was supposed to be this pie-throwing thing with some kids, some teenagers, and I went out there to shoot it.

I said, "Mike, when are you going to do

that?" He said, "We're not. I wrote it out of the script." I said, "Well, it's a shame to have these three pies sitting here and doing nothing with them." He looked up at Harry and said, "I'll take care of that." I said, "What do you mean?" He said, "Just be ready to take your picture."

Mike threw a pie in his face, and I shot it all. But Mike loved Harry; that's why he did it. The whole cast and crew liked Mike because he played jokes on them and you could play a joke on Mike. But he would stop production for ten minutes, tell jokes, and go back to work again.

The crew worked their butts off for him. They loved him.

MICHAEL LED HIS PEOPLE, FOR THE MOST PART, WITH encouragement, humor, and a remarkable intuitive understanding of what worked best on every level of television production. The crew, in general, seemed to work on a very loose tether. Landon had a genuine appreciation for his partner and for their employees, and his pride in their professional excellence inspired them to work their damnedest for him. The word *works* is often used in the film industry to describe any device, technique, or effect that creates an artistically satisfying result. As the boss, Michael Landon knew what worked best for his company—and what allowed him the room to expand so that the resulting creation also worked best.

Michael's singular genius for directing could transform apparently ordinary scripted scenes into compelling and poignant drama. He seldom, if ever, I believe, allowed himself to function by the mechanics of directing alone. The scene that evolved on camera was something that first involved him and his own subconscious identification with the work.

As tuned in as he was to his company, Michael could mentally withdraw from the distractions of a busy set and suddenly retreat to an inward sanctuary to seek only his own counsel. His people understood this and left him alone at such times, confident in the belief that his contemplation would inevitably lead to creative inspiration.

~

There appears to be a great deal of directorial symbolism in your work. Since you invest so much caring energy in crafting images, does it ever bother you that so much of this visual lyricism may often go unnoticed by the casual television viewer?

LANDON: No, it doesn't. Everybody's gotta glean something out of a show. And a lot of times it's just what they're capable of gleaning. There are some people who are just incapable of picking up on certain things like that, because it just isn't part of them. So it doesn't bother me.

Do you do it for yourself and creative fulfillment?

LANDON: Yeah!

You mentioned that inspiration can transport you to this higher realm during your writing and that whole sequences can be composed in that different consciousness. Does that ever happen when you're directing?

LANDON: In the last—jeez, I can't even figure out the number of years—I've given it an opportunity to happen. If you're doing animation, I guess, it's important to have a storyboard, and by God, it certainly worked well for a lot of people. I mean Alfred Hitchcock was not a bum. And many other directors work that way. But for me to try to work with a storyboard and stick to a storyboard—in order to keep all that stuff, to allow it to happen, I don't plan anywhere near like I used to. First of all, I think if you totally plan—and I've seen it happen to a lot of young guys, directors, and some who are much older—the moment one thing happens that isn't exactly as it's planned on the sheet, great problems arise.

For me now, I like to go in the morning earlier and just be on the set, think of my people living there, and I rely on this instinct or whatever it is to take over. And keep it *very* flexible so it changes all the time.

Sometimes what you plan turns out to be an embarrassment when you really get into it. And suddenly things just happen. Yeah, I think I'm open for all that stuff.

I think you're certainly at a point now when you can trust your instincts.

LANDON: Because I know I'm not gonna wander around

the set for two-and-a-half hours without getting the shot. I'm very secure in that way, I know. I could come in and just go ahead and shoot, and I could preplan it, and a lot of times I will preplan it, and I'll walk on the set when it's *quiet*, and I'll feel family people in there.

I'll feel this cast and where they are, and I really want to tell them where I want them to go. I don't want them to have to try to do my job. I'm very secure in moving people and telling them where I think this works and where it doesn't work, and if I'm wrong we'll change it.

Some of the actors that you've worked with have commented to me about that. Pam Roylance was saying that she remembers— it's funny how things stick vividly in certain people's minds— when she was doing "Little House" that she came up to you and was in a quandary. She said, "I actually interrupted him. But he waited and listened to me and heard me out and gave me his entire attention, and then in a few words he answered my question and solved my problem." She said it was wonderful—it was great to work with a director like that.

LANDON: But that's my job. That's my job.

Well, now at this point you are giving yourself license to do more spontaneous visualizing in your directing as well. Trusting to your instincts . . .

LANDON: I used to chew my tongue all the time when I directed. I just had this raw piece of meat in my mouth. But in a more secure fashion, I think I'm going back to not

On the set of "Bonanza" (top left to lower right): Michael Landon,
Dan Blocker, Lorne Greene, Pernell Roberts.
(Photo courtesy of Gene Trindl)

Celebrating St. Valentine's Day on "Little House on the Prairie" in 1975 (left to right): Melissa Sue Anderson, Michael, Melissa Gilbert, and Lindsay Greenbush (front). *(Photo courtesy of NBC)*

Landon passes the pie to Harry Flynn on the set of "Highway to Heaven." *(Photo courtesy of Gene Trindl)*

"Highway to Heaven" actress Maureen Flannigan with author Tom Ito.

Michael's daughter Leslie in schoolteacher's costume on the set of "Little House: A New Beginning." *(Photo courtesy of Pamela Roylance)*

Michael Landon with Pamela Roylance on location for "Little House: A New Beginning." *(Photo courtesy of Pamela Roylance)*

Cinematographer Brianne Murphy with Emmy in her home.

Patricia Neal from
the "Little House on
the Prairie" two-part
episode "Remember Me."
(Photo courtesy of NBC)

Melissa Gilbert and Michael Landon on the set of "Little House."
(Photo courtesy of NBC)

Landon and Victor
French in a scene
from "Little House
on the Prairie."
(Photo courtesy of NBC)

Robert Caspar and
Melissa Gilbert in a
scene from "Little
House on the Prairie."
(Photo courtesy of
Robert Caspar)

Publicity shot from *Where Pigeons Go to Die*.
(Photo courtesy of Gene Trindl)

Michael with film editor Jerry Taylor working on the footage of *Where Pigeons Go to Die.*

Michael Landon, Jr.,
on the set of *Us*.

Michael and author
Tom Ito on the set
of *Us*.

Landon with wife Cindy, son Sean, and daughter Jennifer.
(Photo courtesy of Gene Trindl)

worrying about what worries everybody in television, which is silence and taking the time to be, really be, real.

I think the public has missed that for a long, long time. Real situations don't come and go easily, really. It's OK to take time. We've speeded up life and solutions so much on television to the point where I think people don't give a shit about anything.

I think they're afraid that if there isn't some kind of sound coming out of the set you'll flick it. But if there is a true human being coming out of the set, I think it's so shocking, people will stay. They didn't tune out *Pigeons*. And I've never done a slower-moving project than *Pigeons* in terms of a two-hour film. I mean there were no giant— there was *nothing* gigantic in what happened.

I think even your narration, the way it was paced, was in harmony with that.

LANDON: Yeah. I was afraid to—[*laughs*]—it's a very short script, you know. The whole script was like eighty-two pages that made a two-hour movie. And I must say [*laughs*], it did worry me for a while. [*Pauses*] I loved it!

You know, I gotta tell you, I, I absolutely loved looking at Art Carney and that boy and all of that simplicity, all of that open love. Then you get all of these people who ask— to me, the silliest questions. I mean all of this happened; this happened to be a true story. But I mean: "Oh, are you trying to tell us that this little boy could pull that wagon?"

Well, hell! I've been in a wagon, and I've got a six-

year-old who pulls the wagon when I'm in it! Everybody—
I felt sorry for them! They were unable to allow themselves
to open up enough personally to admit they were moved
by it. And I *know* they were moved by it. They were moved
by it to a point that it made them upset. And it bothered
them. They got touched, in a world that doesn't do that.
And I've had a lot of them admit it to me.

~

WHERE PIGEONS GO TO DIE WAS THE LAST PROPERTY MI-
chael was to produce for NBC. It was a lovely piece of
filmmaking that perfectly harmonized the exuberant poi-
gnancy of his direction with the lyricism of his screenplay.
Based on a book written by R. Wright Campbell, the story
essentially chronicles a valiant homing pigeon's perilous
odyssey home. While his hopeful owner, a young boy
(played by Robert Hy Gorman), awaits his pet's return, the
youngster struggles resolutely to keep a promise to remove
his stricken grandfather (played by Art Carney) from the
ignominy of the hospital to spend his final days with
dignity at home.

Michael was extremely proud of that film, and I think
he believed the picture marked a kind of professional summit. In 1990 it received two Emmy nominations. He at-
tended the ceremonies with his wife, Cindy, but did not
carry a statuette home that evening. It would be his final
appearance at such an event.

"Michael was able to present his creativity through his gut. A lot more directly than a lot of us."

HARRY FLYNN

9

NO INNER LIMITS

THERE WERE TIMES WHEN I BELIEVED THAT HARRY FLYNN must have been one of the busiest press agents in the television business. His functions as a publicist were so integrated with Michael Landon's professional and home life that he seemed constantly absorbed in the whole energetic scope of his client's personal and public endeavors.

Harry's job—managing Michael's public image for the last eight years of the star's life—was not the easiest of tasks because of his client's myriad complexities and intensely private nature. Moreover, Landon was tremendously strong-willed, even intractable regarding the issues and individuals with which he chose to become involved. "If it was yes, then that yes would stand consistently," Harry once remarked to me. "If it was no, then forget it. He could be like a rock. There was no way."

Michael's vehement nature seemed to suit Harry just

fine. I often got the feeling that he thrived on the creative velocity of Michael's temperament. Gentle, scholarly, and mild-mannered, Harry was the perfect foil for Michael's raucous, bawdy humor and an earnest adjutant of his client's maverick integrity.

In turn, I believe, Michael had great respect for his publicist's experience and intuitive professionalism. I have seen the give-and-take in the often hasty conferences that they shared. Michael often readily accepted, evidently without misgivings, Flynn's earnest counsel and tactful input regarding publicity commitments. It was a good relationship. They both did their jobs well and had a hell of a good time doing it.

HARRY FLYNN: There was a kind of antinomy within Michael that was never really satisfied or resolved. He worked enormously hard all of his life. When he wasn't on the soundstage, he spent a tremendous amount of time in the editing room, first learning and later supervising. He did commit an incredible amount of time to his career because he wanted it to be full of achievements. He knew where he was going and he got there.

But that never took from the family in the sense that, as Michael Jr. has said in numerous interviews, he was always there for every athletic contest. For every event of importance for the kids, Michael would be there. You don't do that without a great deal of effort. I know, as a father of several, that takes some scheduling and some doing. And when you're as busy as Michael was, that must have been a herculean task.

He was a very private man in a lot of ways, but I don't know how he ever had much time for himself, because he spent himself so much for the shows to make them what they were and for his kids to make them what they were.

Michael sometimes called himself a blue-collar kind of guy. He was never a star to the crew or to the other actors on the set or to any of us who worked with him. In a way, however, the term *blue-collar* doesn't do justice to the incredible pinnacle that he had achieved creatively.

Blue-collar connotes going to a job, punching a time clock, and just doing the same thing. He was never that way. But he was one of the people that would gather after work and have a beer with the guys before going home; he was blue-collar in that way.

~

Do you believe that a person is destined to a particular purpose in life to achieve something?

LANDON: Oh, I guess you could call it that. I think people

are given certain extraordinary gifts that are very unexplainable. I'm not Ernest Hemingway, but just the fact that I was given the facility to write and to visualize things—all those things are very hard to explain. I mean I can sit down and write stuff, and I write everything in longhand, and my secretary types it up and then gives it to me. And I'll have whole sequences that I have no memory of ever writing. I'm very surprised sometimes at what I've written. *Very* surprised. It's only through my writing that I realized that I'm a very religious person. Because I always had a *great* anger for organized religion because of the terrible problems that it created in my own home, with my mother and father. I mean I was raised in such prejudice. My mother *hated* Jews, and my father did not like Catholics. [*Laughs a little*] Why the hell they ever got married I don't know. They never did tell me that. I'm glad they did, however.

You learn things about yourself when you write. An awful lot of things happen when you're writing that are not consciously going on. You—that—disappears at certain times, and the pencil just goes.

I always thought that part of being human was having the desire to create something. And having the desire to create something is what is really meant by being created in the image of God. Do you understand what I mean?

LANDON: Yes! Very much so.

There's a great deal being said these days about building a "prosperity consciousness." In Discover the Power Within You, *Eric Butterworth wrote: "There is no absence of God in the Universe, and there is no shortage in God. The only lack in life is the thought of lack. You are always as rich as you think you are, and the only poverty is of the spirit." Have the great success and wealth that you've generated come from the longtime belief that it was always out there for you to claim?*

LANDON: I have to be honest: if we're really talking about just the loot and the fact that I make a lot of money, that hasn't altered my life one iota except that I have far more relatives than I ever had before [*laughs*] who are not doing as well as I think they should be. I'm not so sure that I didn't feel as an artist more fulfilled in some of the much poorer financial times than I do now, because I was lucky enough to be working at an age that I thought television was just extraordinary.

A chance to work with the best of writers, Reginald Rose, the best of directors and producers on live television, where—and again, maybe it's just being naive or something—you really felt you were moving multitudes of people. I don't know if I'm even answering your question.

I don't believe the prosperity that you've generated is manifest just in the money. And I don't think that was the sole motivation either.

LANDON: Well, it wasn't for what I did. Not for the shows I picked! Because I think I probably could have picked some easier shots. Although I think I'm being led in all of my career work. There'll be a lot of people who will probably listen to that and say, "Sss, religious fanatic stuff."

Led in the sense that you are being guided?

LANDON: Led *and* guided! Why would I want to pick each time things that no one wanted to do and yet that I really believed if I did them properly and did what I should do—because I'm not self-destructive—would be successful? I just didn't listen to what I was told from Madison Avenue and from the network.

Part of the abundance has been in your great wellspring of creativity. You've written, you've directed, you've done this all so consistently well. That's a wealth in itself: not to have exhausted that and start turning out hack and mediocre work. Bri and some of the folks that I've had a chance to talk with that worked with you feel that you've not only been consistently good but continue to improve.

LANDON: I think only because I've gotten into a position where I'm not stopped from doing it—and I think there's a lot of other people that could do it. I think there's a lot of terrific people out there who never get an opportunity because they don't know how to make a piece of crap.

When you're handed a piece of crap, if you gotta make a living you gotta make a piece of crap. Any show that you know is terrible, but you know is going to get a number—that's what *everybody* is up against.

And it's generally the lowest common denominator.

Not something that improves life or improves the relation-ships between human beings—I mean that's why we end up with a whole generation of guys who haven't the slight-est idea of what women are about. Of what love is about.

We've been handed role models that are the worst of all, and everybody has to live up to it! Because apparently that's everybody. It's *not* everybody. I think it's a real small proportion of the public—if the public was honest. I mean, that's why cocaine fulfills a great desire for love and covers and coats. Just a very, very sad, insecure lifestyle we have now.

Perhaps part of the salvation of your prosperity has been the courage to do it your own way. You created your own shows, you fought for them, you've always insisted upon control.

LANDON: But I got lucky enough to get in a position to do it. You know if I had bad numbers I never would have done that. You *know*.

~

You previously remarked that it was through your writing that you discovered that you were a very religious man. Was this a gradual realization or a sudden revelation?

LANDON: I think it was gradual. The first few times—and I'm not alone in that obviously—that my subconscious wrote and shocked me when I read it, always being this solid human being, I pretended that I was just going so fast that I didn't remember it. But too much has happened since that time. Too many things have been written by me and many other people that make you sit back and realize that there are moments in everyone's life when a much stronger hand takes your pencil. And it scares me to a certain extent . . .

Scared in the sense that it frightens you or that it awes you?

LANDON: It awes me and can become a terrible crutch, because then you say, "Well, when are you taking my hand again? [*Laughs*] Are you busy right now?"

In a way I think it's a good question to ask. I think it's actually a form of prayer. And it's a very legitimate appeal. It does have its answer, because it does come to you in its own good time.

LANDON: Yeah.

IN 1973, AT THE AGE OF SEVENTEEN, LANDON'S STEP-daughter Cheryl suffered critical injuries in an automobile accident. Michael later related in an article in *Life* magazine that while praying for her recovery at her bedside he had resolved to do something meaningful with his life. He always believed her recovery to be a great miracle.

HARRY FLYNN: I think there was an inner core of truth that Michael believed in. I don't know if it started when he made the promise when Cheryl was very sick after the automobile accident or whether he had always had a desire to tell the truth as he knew it through his medium, which was television. I don't know. But he had an inner guide like an inertial guidance system in a rocket that had unerring good taste in terms of what he wanted to do.

To say that it wasn't his creativity, I guess, is not accurate, because it's like saying there's not much use in putting the inertial guidance system in a little boat with a sail on it that you're going to sail in a pond. You put it in a giant missile that's going to go somewhere, because it takes a whole lot of hardware to go that far. So you have to have the propellant to send the missile.

I think he always had within an inner good taste that kept him from straying off the path of where he wanted to go, which was to present some very honest entertainment. I think he wanted to present *honesty* as he knew it, and the dramatic form was his method of expressing himself best. I think something kept him very honest.

Michael was able to present his creativity through his gut. A lot more directly than a lot of us. He didn't have to search for it; it was there. He had opened the avenues to creativity when a lot of us aren't able to. And some artists, writers, painters, and all drink or do other things to loosen them up. He didn't have to do that because he was there. It was like the wellspring was close to the source. I think maybe it was confidence. He had total confidence in what was within him to speak the truth, and it never let him down.

"I wanted people to listen and did it in the wrong way. As soon as I got more secure, I didn't have to do that. Not secure financially, but as a person."
                                                    MICHAEL LANDON

10

ON DEMONS AND DOUBTS

MICHAEL LANDON, SINCE HIS DEATH, HAS BEEN CANON-
ized by many of the same people who once censured him
in a succession of highly colored formula articles that
labeled him as arrogant, self-righteous, haughtily aloof,
and dictatorial. Stories of his alleged temper tantrums and
punishing sarcasm toward hapless reporters were also a
common staple for entertainment publications throughout
much of the fifteen years that Landon produced his two
television series. Even a perusal of some of the many *TV
Guide* articles written about him reveals that profiles were
often patronizing and tinged with disapproval.

In "First Rule of the 'Prairie': Michael Landon Must
Have Control" (January 9–15, 1982), for example, Mary
Murphy sketched a portrait dismayingly at variance with

the compassionate character Landon played on "Little House":

> I wanted to ask Michael Landon about his devils. I also wanted to ask him, since "Little House" could be in its final year, what he will do next. It took almost three months for the elusive Landon to find time to talk, and even then he would talk only on the run. Finally, when he refused to allow a formal interview, I said to him in frustration, "Ingmar Bergman talked to me for eight hours."
>
> "Ingmar Bergman," Landon snapped, "has eight hours. I do not."

Journalists seemed to find Landon perversely complex, and what they wrote often mirrored the frustration that stemmed from their thwarted attempts to get a handle on the man. Michael Leahy wrote in *TV Guide* in March 1985:

> Of course, as with anyone whose life has been a roller coaster of cataclysms and major triumphs, he has layers beneath layers, and few people are privy to all of them. Get too close, and all you see are the contradictions. The moralist who talks incessantly about the need for "strong family values" is the temperamental artist on his third marriage to a woman 20 years younger. The benefactor who has quietly paid the unexpected hospital bills of some crew members is the petu-

lant star who mocked Priscilla Presley, his co-star in a Thailand-based 1983 movie called *Love Is Forever*, for taking so much time to comb her hair in the fetid humidity of Bangkok. The man who sits out of view from auditioning actors so as not to make them nervous (He *hates* readings," says his casting director, Susan McCray. "I think he feels sorry for some of these people. It reminds him of his old days") is the same one who, in Bangkok, during *Love Is Forever*, arrogantly shot some of his own scenes without authorization from either the director or the cinematographer.

IN *US* MAGAZINE (JUNE 15, 1987), MARK MORRISON EMphasized Michael's hotheadedness during his early years as an actor, which could lead to out-and-out brawls:

"Everyone wanted to say they punched out a Cartwright," [Landon] remembers. Young and defiant, he was happy to oblige.

There was also sparring of another kind on the set. Despite its blockbuster ratings, "Bonanza" wasn't "Playhouse 90." Landon was no longer finding satisfaction as an actor. "This is a piece of crap," he would tell the director.

Michael was the favorite fall guy for a lot of journalistic ax grinding by reporters who apparently reveled in caricaturing his outspokenness on his political stands, his maverick personality, and his unabashed romanticism. I believe that his extreme self-confidence and intensity—qualities that he never lost—often intimidated and sometimes baffled people less certain of their personal and creative convictions. As an independent producer, he was extremely sure of his own professional ability in an industry that is filled with insecure people often hampered by a very narrow range of ability.

Michael's professional creed definitely included insistence on creative control over his projects. He knew the value of efficient structure and believed in assuming responsibility for that structure. This adamance drew a lot of fire from numerous Landon-phobes, who were happy to infer that he was suppressive. Landon himself undoubtedly would have responded simply with what he said to me on more than one occasion: "I don't want to have someone else feel that they have to do my job."

"There was an attitude about Michael, in the industry," Brianne Murphy once told me. "When people found out you had worked for him, they automatically assumed you were spoiled, because Mike treated us all very well. I think there was a great deal of jealousy over that and over his strong-willed insistence that he do things his own way." That attitude often translated into rough handling by the press, and Michael, I sensed, was hardly indifferent to the controversy he sparked. It affected him deeply, but he was a prideful individual. Despite his open emotionalism with intimates, he could be a stoic to strangers and was understandably quite wary with reporters.

None of this tension ever arose in our relationship,

however. Michael was nothing if not totally frank. Rather than being recalcitrant, he actually encouraged the rapport, for he possessed the self-confident gregariousness of a man solidly on his own successful ground. In fact his open candor revealed that he could be extremely moved by the phenomenon of friendship.

HARRY FLYNN: It's hard for me to think of him as a prickly character. I guess he was tougher to deal with as a kid. He was feisty, and he was anxious to get ahead, and it's a tough business. He was ready to fight always for what he believed in, but I never saw the prickly character myself.

I only worked with him the last eight years of his life; he was very gracious, I always thought. And I'm sure you saw the same person. He was very knowledgeable, and it was hard for me to believe that he wasn't always as amiable and gentle as he was when I knew him. He was terribly sensitive and very fun. Always a warm, very loving person inside.

So I never saw that difficult part. I knew there were times when he was quite adamant about taking a stand, particularly an ethical stand, but that didn't make him a tough person to get along with. I always felt that he was marvelous to work with, and that never changed.

~

One of the impressions I came away with from our first meeting was that you have achieved self-mastery, which is an impression one rarely gets from anyone.

LANDON: Well, I'm sure a hell of a lot more mellow now. But see, [in the early days] I was arguing in a different way. When you argue with no power base, you learn early up, if I'm gonna get anywhere, sometimes I've gotta get on the case! Because otherwise nobody's gonna listen. Once you have a power base, and people say, "Shit, he was right there, he was right there, he was right there," then they'll listen. The point is, *no one was listening.* Like, when I was Little Joe, nobody was listening. So I *would* say outrageous things.

I didn't get along with him [Kent McCray]. My partner. Phew! We hated each other! Oh, it was terrible! We had some real knock-down, drag-out fights! But when I look back on that, quite obviously since he's still my partner, I can very easily see—and knew at that time—that that was only because I was insecure. I wanted people to listen and did it in the wrong way. As soon as I got more secure, I didn't have to do that. Not secure financially, but as a person.

~

You mentioned that you would like your legacy to be that you were remembered as a good guy to work for. I think those were almost your exact words.

LANDON: Yeah, and, you know, I might want to alter that to work *with*. [*Laughs*] Not to say that I'm going to change my mind, because I found myself on many occasions, especially with actors, probably taking a devious route to being correct. But not for all the wrong reasons, for the reasons that I may have been caught momentarily. And I don't want them to believe that they're not contributing.

I've always found that in any kind of organization there is almost a definite need for one singular voice, at least in looking at the overall picture of what you want to have when you're done. And I'm very flexible in that way, but I'm flexible in a way where people won't think I'm flexible. If you understand what I mean.

I don't want to lose control of anything. Not out of egotistical reasons, but because if *they* want to make it, then they should make one too, and they should make it the way they like to make it.

It's like looking at the things that you write. When I first started writing, people who directed my writing did not do a bad job. They did a very, very good job. It was just a *different* job. Their idea of what the important moment was was totally different from my idea of what the important moment was.

You could take the same script and have ten very

talented people direct it, and you could have ten entirely different, albeit ten entertaining, projects. But if you're the original writer of it, it's *never* the same. And I know that. I feel very badly when I take another guy's piece of work sometimes—I was so thrilled on *Pigeons* when I finally met the writer at Melissa Sue Anderson's wedding. I'd never met the man—not because I didn't want to meet him, but he lives in the woods and I live here. And I was *thrilled* that he was happy.

I was concerned with NBC wanting to change the title of his book. I didn't want them to change it. I'm not saying *Where Pigeons Go to Die* is the kind of title that's gonna get everybody tuning in, but I think I owe him that. My God! His product is what moved me, so it's not my right to change his title.

~

In one particular episode of "Highway" your character, Jonathan, advised a troubled man believing himself to be King Arthur that our sorrows sometimes come from being out of balance in our desires and ambitions. Have you ever had to face that challenge?

LANDON: You know, I'm so shocked that I ever got this successful. I really am. I was always happy wherever I was as long as I could make a living for my family. For me, making a living in this business was the ultimate because I love doing it. I love the business itself.

And the only difference was how big your yard was.

You know what I'm saying? If you're making x amount of bucks, you've got a bigger yard, but that doesn't mean that you're gonna have more fun in that yard than you had in any sandlot you ever played on—as long as everybody was doing it together. There are a lot of big empty lots around.

That's probably not an answer to your question.

In a way it's a very good answer. For the lots are kind of symbolic of a lot of lives too. The answer, I suppose, is that you always have in your own way retained that balance out of an innate sense of modesty. [A pause]

It's strange. I find it the most curious thing, especially after we did our first interview. When I had all the collection of TV Guide *articles and things, I was just bewildered by how many times the adjective* arrogant *had been applied to you.*

LANDON: I've always been amazed! I guess apparently what that has to do with is, when I work I'm secure. I'm very secure in what I do. I am good at what I do. And therefore I don't have to scream. It's like a parent. You're secure in what you do. And you've got it together. You don't have to scream, you don't have to beat—that's insecurity that causes all that.

That's what I was downtown about today [speaking out about foster-home program reforms]: hopefully, spending a few more of the state's and county's dollars on keeping families together instead of pulling kids and putting them into foster homes. I mean there's a lot of parents out there. They don't want to lose their kids, and God knows the kids don't want to lose their parents.

[*Sighs*] You could beat the hell out of a kid, and that kid does not want to leave the mother and father. So, let's work on the front end instead of the back. No, I'm very secure in what I do, and I don't think that's arrogant.

I read it all the time myself. I think if one person writes it, it's like . . .

Like a buzzword?

LANDON: Oh, sure. It's a buzzword. It's like that silly biography that that woman wrote. I mean, all she did was take articles out of the *National Enquirer* and every other publication she could find and put 'em down and make a buck with my picture on the cover. And I'll be honest with you, I haven't read the book. And I understand that there's nothing terrible in the book. And I don't know one way or the other because I haven't read it.

I can remember reading a cover on *TV Guide* about these deep dark horrendous demons in the back of my life. Shit! I don't think any of the people I've worked with for twenty-five years know where these deep dark demons are. Shit! We all sit around. It's like sitting in an editing room. I win some, I lose some. I like what I do.

"You know, I sat up to sometimes two or three in the morning. Because every once in a while I'll get guilty. I'll feel guilty. Why haven't I turned out more product? Because I'm so used to turning out all of the stuff. And I thought, Well, it just hasn't been the right time."

MICHAEL LANDON

11

ILLUMINATIONS

I FIND IT IRONIC THAT SO MANY OF THE TRIBUTES EXTOL-ling the humanity and work of Michael Landon have been posthumous. Much of the publicity that dogged the man when he was alive was flatly critical, and his shows were often dismissed by reviewers as being juvenile and banal. Michael once remarked that critics seemed to spend more time reviewing his hair than his work.

Landon possessed tremendous charisma, but like any form of magnetism his seemed to attract certain individuals and repel others, with equal intensity. Michael, I believe, knew very well that his having remained distinctly on the periphery of mainstream Hollywood society and its vanity circuit, despite an amazing thirty-year career, made him a kind of anomaly in the business. He followed his own muse, and this quest often led him to a solitary realm beyond the clamor of sycophancy.

A great measure of this reticence, I believe, also issued from basic shyness. Michael was not an intrusive man, and by the same token he disliked outsiders—particularly certain members of the press who exaggerated his intractibility—encroaching beyond what he perceived as being the public boundaries of his life.

Landon's sensitive style of acting and his vibrant, self-confident public image were but partial expressions of a meditative man living out of his own center. This was the personal substance from which he drew creative energy and with which he availed himself of artistic inspiration. It was also a realm in which he contended with the dark images that can dwell within any person's past and with which he felt compelled to make peace.

Behind the parapet of wariness he had thrown up against public intrusion dwelled an individual of resolute candor. I recall an occasion when Michael and I sat together for about an hour while he read the draft copy of a manuscript I had written profiling him. I'd been warned by skeptical acquaintances that he would riddle the pages with revisions in blue ink. Instead, he read in silence for about fifteen minutes and then asked quietly, "Do you have a pen?" I handed it to him and he made a single notation on the printout: in tiny letters, he wrote his father's name, "Eli," above where I had mistakenly typed "Sam." The silence resumed until after about forty-five minutes, he turned the final page, lit a cigarette, and tersely delivered to me my happiest literary compliment. "Beautiful," he remarked with quiet brevity. "Brilliant."

We then taped a conversation of some fairly personal material, some of it included here. "I'll make sure that you get an updated printout for approval," I assured him when we had finished. "I know this stuff might be sensitive." Michael shrugged. "Don't worry," he told me. "I trust you." That may have been a guileless remark, but Michael had an instinct for human nature. If he trusted you, you would damn near kill to protect that trust.

There can sometimes occur in friendship, I believe, a moment when an unspoken pact of mutual acceptance is sealed. Whatever was said or done up to that moment of agreement is simply the prelude to the realization of friendship. I believe that such acceptance came from Michael late one afternoon in Malibu during that second taped interview. We had just closed a lengthy conversation, only a portion of which was taped. Michael had seemed particularly pensive that day, and his remarks often reflected his introspection. Whether offhanded and chatty or deeply reflective, his words were conveyed with forthright candor.

I have heard certain actors declare the opinion that Landon was an individual exceptionally without fear. I disagree. Michael, like anyone, had his own fears, and he very well knew what many of them were. What *was* exceptional was how he dealt with them: he seldom, if ever, let them get in the way of what he felt he needed to do, and that, I think, is the basis of all personal valor.

Behind the mask of celebrity and the polished facade of a worldly public figure accustomed to dispatching interviews with precision and reserve abided a spirit of poignant innocence and naive wonder. Michael carried within himself, I believe, a sanctuary of childlike idealism. It was a refuge for an uninhibited, naive soul fascinated with personal magic.

This realm was the source of both Landon's genius and his humanity. Work was the most dynamic channel for their expression. For those who knew him in unguarded and silent moments of friendship, however, the shared intimacy of his secret simplicity was an ultimate expression of love.

~

You project the image of being a very strong and controlled individual. How have you been able to maintain that difficult balance of protecting yourself from callous encroachments upon your personal sovereignty and at the same time preserving the sensitivity of a caring and creative man?

LANDON: I think mainly it's because when my business day is over, my business day is over. I don't carry my work around. It doesn't make or break my day. I mean I'd rather have a terrific day at work, but a lousy day is just one of those days, and it's over. What's going on in your house and your personal life and your own family is far more important than what you do for a living, no matter how much you like doing it.

Well, you've had to deal with a lot of, I would imagine, circuses too. I mean just beyond the periphery of your work, being creative, you run into a lot of exploitive factors.

LANDON: Oh, yeah, but that's been going on for so many years that it's very easy for me not to be involved in those things. I don't socialize a great deal anyway. I have a very small group of friends. Actually none of my real close friends are in this business.

So, it's hard to exploit me because it's hard to find me. [*Laughs*] I'm generally working. When I'm working you can find me, but otherwise I'm at home.

What about the stress of success itself? How do you deal with that?

LANDON: I don't have any. I absolutely don't have any. I just enjoy working. I mean I really like it when I work. For the first time in my life I also like it now, when I *don't* work. That's fun too. I don't feel as obligated to work constantly, because I know my people are all the best, so they're all gonna get jobs right away anyway. I used to be worried about keeping everybody together constantly. You can't do that. It's just too tough.

Have you achieved peace of mind?

LANDON: [*Reflects for a moment*] Yeah. I think so. We're all gonna have a different amount of peace of mind, I suppose. I don't think you ever get away from a lot of images that stay with you from your childhood—a lot of strange little things that are always there that affect you later.

I'm not tolerant when it comes to complaining. I'm not tolerant when it comes to even complaining about physical ailments. It's just one of those things that I'm left with. My mother with all her other insanity was also a hypochondriac, so I can't—I mean, there's certain things that you just live with.

I can't stand people talking about astrology. It irritates me to death! Because again, my mother was into that, and if it said in the newspaper, you're gonna have a bad day, by God, my mother had a bad day, and so did everybody else! So all these things stay with you. But in terms of overall peace of mind, I think I have that.

We spoke about dreams providing a positive force and direction in life. What about nightmares? Have you ever had to make your peace with dark images?

LANDON: Do you know what I have terrible dreams about occasionally? And I'm not talking about sleeping dreams. But there are times in your life when you've thrown something out with a group of people you're with, especially when guys are together, that has turned out to hurt people. And I know everybody does. *Why* I have this I don't know, because I think it's time to shed it. But I have a recurring thing about a girl.

One night when I was seventeen years old or something, we were driving in a car. The guys would occasionally use me to pick up girls, because I was a baby-faced kind of a guy, nonaggressive-looking type with a semi-good personality. So they would pop me out of a car door if two girls were walking down the street, and I would strike up the conversation in an attempt to pick up a couple of girls. We'd get to neck with them, you know, or buy them a hamburger.

It was the wintertime, and I popped out of the car, and there were two girls walking, and one girl was extraordinarily beautiful. She had a scarf on her head. We started talking as we walked along the block, and the one girl had blond hair. I said to the girl with the scarf on, "What color is your hair?" And she—I know this is stupid for me to tell you this—she said, "Oh, who cares?" And I said, "Well, what's the matter? Are you bald?" And I pulled her scarf down. And she *was* bald!

I gotta tell you, I have *never*—I don't think there's a month that goes by—because what I did was run away. It scared me! I felt so awful that I said that. And I know how devastating that must have been for her that I did that.

Isn't that a strange thing to tell you? I'm not quite sure why I'm telling you. But I've never forgotten that and how much I wish I had stayed and just talked about what it was, so she'd see that it wasn't so awful. You know, whether it was alopecia or she—it was prior to chemo, I think. Ah, she may have had some of that, but I would imagine it was alopecia.

That's always bothered me, all these years.

That kind of thoughtfulness, though, has been a theme in a lot of your shows. Characters sort of thoughtlessly do something, unintentionally hurt somebody, realize it, and then try to make good by it. In a way, maybe it was a good thing. I mean, not certainly . . .

LANDON: I know what you're saying. And there's a number of things, and I know there's gotta be a number of those things in your life too.

Sure. I remember one time, my family had a parakeet, and I really loved that bird. One day, I pushed the swinging kitchen door on the bird. I knew exactly the moment that it was gone. And I pushed it and it just went down. It was dead.

LANDON: Oh, it was devastating!

And to this day, I . . .

LANDON: You remember!
    I can remember picking up my uncle's goldfish. Why I did it I don't know. I didn't want to hurt it. I picked it up, and when I picked it up, it folded up! I guess I squeezed it when I picked it up. And I put it back in, and it was like an L shape. I was doing that shit, and I lied to my aunt and uncle. I said, "I don't know what happened to it. I guess it died."
    I can remember walking home from school with a bunch of kids, and you know how there'll be a whole bunch of birds on a lawn? And how you want to scare the

birds away? I picked up a rock and threw the rock, hit the bird on the head, and killed it! It was one of so many birds. I felt awful!

But apparently we were bonded! We have some kind of—there must be some kind of feelings that some people have that are a different . . .

We go through certain kinds of martyrdoms in our memory. And it's part of our formation. It increases our sensitivity in certain areas. So in a way, I think that martyrdom is a good thing. It sensitizes us in a good way.

LANDON: Sure!

~

Has there been a particular summit in your life, or is there one yet ahead of you?

LANDON: Oh, I think that would vary. I think everybody's mountain range would probably look different. For some it would be what appeared to be a mountain and became a plateau, and that's great. It's comfortable and can be beautiful, and there are lovely plateaus in this world. For some of us it's up one side of a mountain and down the other and into a valley—maybe more highs and lows in terms of sadness and happiness. But I think everybody's mountain range is already there when we come into this world.

111

Destiny?

LANDON: Yeah! I think a hand draws all those figures.

Are you still climbing?

LANDON: I've gone through a very strange period of non-productiveness in terms of a product. But I don't think it's nonproductiveness in terms of really getting my life and its priorities together for what I'm gonna do from now on. I'm about to enter into some big changes. I've never been affiliated with a major company before, and I have a feeling within the next week or so, I will be [with CBS].

But as much as it makes everybody here nervous—and I continue to carry all these people, so that's been my style—I've really enjoyed this last year and a half, without having to do anything. I have to get myself away from the obligation of keeping everybody working all the time, because I'm not *the only* person in town. You trap yourself into an obligation to make everybody's job.

I love all the people, but I can't just make something because I want them to work, because I'm not satisfied. I'm dissatisfied. I could put together a television series now. I mean I could do it in maybe five minutes. Yes, I'll do a series, it'll start in September, and I'll show it to you when it's done. But that just isn't what I want to do anymore.

I've read one thing that I really definitely want to do and that I'm gonna do. It's not written by me. I think it's a terrific piece. It's about victims. Every story that you see about some kind of horrendous crime, they always do the court and the trial and what happens to the bad guy. This is solely about the family, so that people can see what happens.

I don't want to feel that I have to make a product just for the sake of making a product so that I'll provide the job. Because all my people are working. They're the best in town. They're doing great. I'd rather do some features and some specials, and if a series comes along that looks like it would really be fun to do, then I'll do it.

It's also given me a chance to get back to what I needed to do, and that's physically take care of myself. I'll guarantee you that if you are physically working out and your body is feeling the way God made you feel—aside from my terrible vices [*nods toward his cigarettes*], because I don't want to live to be ninety-five anyway, you know; I just want to look good for viewers [*we laugh*]—I am so much smarter when I'm working out, and I'm strong. I'm up every morning, work out in this gym at six-thirty. I've got my tennis lesson at seven o'clock in the morning, twice a week. For me as a physical human being, that makes me smart. I got into a slouch of feeling bad about myself physically. The blood wasn't moving enough. You *must* feel that way—come on. It's like when the endorphins are rolling, you're feeling good.

I think that, first of all, it shows creative integrity—which pretty much marks your whole career anyway. . . .

LANDON: I spent a great deal of time thinking it was fear. [*Laughs*] Which would not be uncommon. Let's face it, you could take icons, you could take idols and realize that the fear of failure totally destroyed them. There's no better case in point than Orson Welles. I mean, absolutely phenomenal verve and mind and fear. Fear destroyed him.

~

I think with the decisions that you've made—I sensed it anyway—you've reached this plateau.

LANDON: You know, I sat up to sometimes two or three in the morning. Because every once in a while I'll get guilty. I'll feel guilty. Why haven't I turned out more product? Because I'm so *used* to turning out all of the stuff. And I thought, Well, it just hasn't been the right time.

I don't think you'll ever be seduced into the charade of achieving something. The achievement and accomplishment will be grounded in real inspiration. And that'll come.

LANDON: Oh, it's coming now. [*Pauses*] I also have a very funny work ethic. And I've lost it with NBC. See, even though I'm an independent producer, I like the feeling that I have a boss. I've always liked that feeling. And there's a driving force in me that wants to please my boss. [*Points overhead*] Not just that Boss.

NBC doesn't give me that anymore. They just don't give it. It's an accounting company; it's totally changed. And I don't expect people to give me dinners or big pats on the back or anything else. I made a lot of money for that company.

But I am at the point where, for instance, when *Pigeons* was on, *I expect someone to call me.* If he's my boss, then, like what I do with everybody who works for me: I don't give a shit how many people there are, I don't miss a day with the guys, because I love my yard for instance. I have ten acres of beauty, and I love that beauty, and I love the flowers and the big vegetable gardens. I wouldn't miss a day of telling the guys who do my yard what a fucking great job they're doing! "Goddamn, what a great choice of mixing these flowers! Just terrific!" We need that! People need to be encouraged!

I mean my main reason for not being with NBC anymore is only because I'm *tired* of being the shadow. I mean, I'm nonexistent.

Do you know how little it would take? I mean, *one fucking call!* They liked the show, they liked Art Carney, they liked this—

To call me up and say they liked the number, which I didn't even get, wouldn't mean shit to me. But to have them call up and say, "God! I was proud that we had that on!"—that would have meant something to me.

Nobody called?

LANDON: Zip! Zero! Absolutely nothing.

What I believe though, first of all I believe we're on the threshold of a renaissance, as we spoke of earlier. I am convinced, that even though your works have sort of preceded that renaissance, it is a part of your destiny to make a great contribution to the renaissance to come. We're standing right on the threshold, and you've got your finger right on the issues that matter and that would characterize that renewal.

LANDON: Right! [*to Harry, who has just entered the room*] He's gonna come here every day now, at seven o'clock in the morning. I'm gonna lie on the couch, and he's gonna talk to me!

*"Michael was one of the only people that I know in
the film business who was actually and literally
doing it for the pleasure, for the fun of it. He was
doing it because he wanted to do it.*

ROBERT CASPAR

12

PASSION PLAYS

MICHAEL LANDON'S DISCONTENT WITH NBC EVENTU-
ally led to a parting of the ways with the network with
which he had been affiliated for nearly thirty years. It was
a change that he appeared to take philosophically, and
while he contemplated a proposed move to CBS he was
nurturing the seeds of new projects with his customary
restless energy.

As Michael himself has said, money never became the
sole motivation for his professional intensity. The work in
itself was a magnificent obsession to him. What else could
account for his having, as Harry Flynn later noted to me,
logged more than eight hundred hours of airtime as a
performer? I think work fascinated him, and the team
effort of "everybody doing it together," as he once put it,
brought him both self-esteem and fellowship in a uniquely
satisfying and exhilarating manner.

117

Landon's disenchantment with NBC, I believe, was the reaction of an accomplished artist who no longer felt a creative alliance with his employer. The acceptance of his peers and the approval of the network for which he worked were tremendously important to Michael, and the network had failed to pay him the "psychic income" he desired. NBC was the boss Michael had strived to please for three decades, many of his endeavors had given the Peacock some of its brightest programming, and the network had prospered appreciably because of certain Michael Landon productions. He was hurt deeply by the apparent indifference of NBC executives to the high ratings and popular success that Michael had brought them.

That issue was at the front of my mind when Michael and I had our third (and what was to be our final) recorded interview during the early autumn of 1990. His production company was preparing to move its production office from Malibu to the familiar old MGM studio that had been assumed by Columbia. It was a transitional period of great significance in Landon's life. He had been a star for and in essence had grown up on NBC, so I couldn't help wondering if he had misgivings about his defection.

Despite his intense focus on the future, I found him in a distinctly nostalgic mood. Michael, I think, carried within his memory a kind of archive of greatly satisfying artistic summits. It was this chronicle that helped keep alive much of the joy he found in his work.

BRIANNE MURPHY: Working with Mike was a constant learning process. He would do really beautiful things that were absolutely amazing. He could get to a location that to a lot of people would seem quite plain and uninspired, pick a spot for the camera and his actors, and it suddenly became magic. The man was absolutely a genius, and I think he's probably one of the most underrated people in television as far as that creative genius that he had goes.

God knows he was successful—everyone knows that—but I don't think there was anybody around who could have done better work. I learned so much from him. It wasn't in regard so much to specific shots but rather in the larger concept of taking a scene and being able to visualize it. Since I have my own aspirations to direct, I often use what I think would be his methods. It wasn't like he ever sat around and talked about how he did it, so it was a matter of having to be aware of him.

ROBERT CASPAR: Michael was one of the only people that I know in the film business who was actually and literally doing it for the pleasure, for the fun of it. He was doing it because he *wanted* to do it. We had a small conversation one day, and he said, "You know, I retired once." I said, "What the hell did you come back for?" He said, "I got bored."

He literally was working because it was a great, great pleasure. This is something unique in Hollywood, where so many people consider this thing a rat race, something to bring in under time with time limits, mechanical and inhuman. That's why he's going to be greatly missed, because I'm afraid, in my opinion, the business is moving further and further toward mechanization and inhumanness.

Whatever his beliefs and thoughts, he made it possible for all of those people to function as true human beings. It was a very different kind of set. He was also aware that, because of the kind of show it was ["Little House on the Prairie"], it was always creeping toward sentimentality, and he was always aware to counteract that and purposely move into freshness to stay away from that stale sentimental kind of thing.

~

In a past conversation you touched on some new professional changes that you were looking at.

LANDON: All they are are position changes. I'm not going

to be with NBC anymore; I'll be basically with CBS in terms of network affiliation, and I'll also be under contract to Columbia Studios for motion pictures and television.

Well, I imagine that, consistent with your career, those changes are of your own will.

LANDON: Yeah! That's what I pursued. And my long relationship with NBC, in many ways I'm sorry to see it end. Because I really liked a number of the creative people out there. Tartikoff, I think, is a terrific guy, and I've always enjoyed working with him. But it's run in a corporate structure today that has no care whatsoever for loyalty or people who have been with them for a long time.

I mean their attitude in business affairs towards me would be the same as if someone just walked in off the street today. And after over thirty years I'm not gonna take that. I don't think that's right. Therefore I can't do business with them.

~

When we spoke of personal summits, you said that you thought that "a hand draws all those figures," that that terrain is there for us before we even come along and start on our own trails. I was wondering what it was for you. That hand, what did it draw for you?

LANDON: [*Considers several moments before replying*] Gee, I don't know, you know? I'm a strange person. See, for me, when everything is going great, I'm probably at my least happy. Because, I don't know, I guess my whole psyche just kicks back and gets depressed. Do you know what I'm saying?

Yes. I think you need a barrier or a challenge to get the adrenaline going.

LANDON: Yeah! I need that little kick in the tush, I guess. Or to get myself to do it to myself, because you really, you know, have to do it to yourself.

It's like shooting a show if we're doing episodic television. So you're doing a show, and you're doing a show every six days or every five days or whatever your schedule is, and it all goes along, and it all gets done, and you're enjoying it, and everything is fine, but [*shrugs*] so? Then all of a sudden you go to do one, and it's about a drought, and it rains for seven days. And you have to figure out how you can change that show and make it work when it was originally supposed to be a drought and now it's raining for seven days.

Now, you can just shut down and not do anything, except then you'd miss all the excitement, because the excitement is: how do I continue working and make this show terrific and even maybe make it better with all this adversity going on? And that's when I end up having the most fun. That's when Kent has the most fun. He loves that stuff.

Were there certain situations like that you can recall?

LANDON: Oh, sure! The one we did in Arizona. You talk about rain! It was unbelievable! It was just constant rewrite the entire time, and it turned out great. The show turned out to be wonderful.

It was the last year of "Bonanza." We've had a lot of them on "Highway." And in "Little House" we had this beautiful scene—it was such a sad show. These guys were selling diseased cattle. It was killing people. And this father had a scene to do on a hillside in Simi Valley, holding his dead son.

It was supposed to be this *beautiful*, gorgeous day. And he's rocking his son, and he's out of it. He's gone. What he's talking to me about is taking his son on a picnic because it's such a beautiful day. Well, the day we got there, the wind was blowing—it was gusting sixty, seventy miles an hour. I'd never seen a wind like that, and it was *freezing* cold. The sky was just this angry-looking sky. There wasn't a bit of blue anywhere. And dust everyplace!

Everybody was talking about wrapping it up. And I— the actor was shocked. I said, "No! No!" I said, "God, we've gotta shoot it now." I said, "This is perfect!" He said, "But I talk about what a great day for the picnic . . ." I said, "But you're talking about a son who isn't even alive too!" I said, "This isn't what you see or feel. That's all taking place inside you."

The scene was *awesome* that way. And he really didn't want to do it, because the wind was bothering him. I said,

"Then forget the wind. Forget everything. Just hold him!" And God, it was extraordinary! It was wonderful! Those are the days you go home and say, "Whew!"

So there were certain plateaus and peaks during production when it really became a matter of artistry, and it wasn't just something that you were doing as a matter of reflex.

LANDON: Oh, yeah. In other words, would I shoot just to shoot? No! It's when those things happen that you really begin to think. You start thinking on a different level. Instead of the comfort, easy-thinking level, you shift into another gear that's more exciting.

You know, there were times when I would watch your shows, any of the series, and I almost got the feeling that you were getting a providential hand, when the elements were on your side.

LANDON: I know what you're talking about, and our whole crew is in tune to that. Like, a cloud! I mean things that people don't think about in episodic TV: a certain-shaped cloud or just a certain look at that moment. Bing! I mean, we've got a camera *now*! We're ready! You gotta do it *now*. You're not gonna get another shot at that.

Things happen with actors. I had a big long scene in front of the Garvey ranch one time. And it was very expository but very necessary. It was at an outside picnic, a luncheon. And Merlin Olson [who played John Garvey in "Little House"] had a lot of dialogue in it—*everybody* did, to try and advance the story. It was about four-and-a-half pages. We had a baby sitting in a high chair. And it was very warm.

So we put the little plate of food in front of the baby. The baby was about a year old, and the heat got to the baby immediately and made the baby sleepy. I was running two cameras, but I had one of them on, I think it was Caroline, on Karen Grassle, because she had a lot of the dialogue in the first take, and I had a master. So I tapped him right away when we started the scene, because I could see the baby nodding off.

We panned over real quick, and I took a nice shot of the baby—a nice eye shot. We ended up playing probably half of the scene of all this dialogue on the baby. Because, well, you've seen people starting to nap, when they're sitting up, and then they'll get down, down, down . . . [*Lowers his head and then jerks it up*] . . . and then it'll go like this. Well, those kinds of things, they never come again. So you kind of jump on them.

~

Are there times when, just as a performer, you're enthralled and you deliver a great, inspired piece of acting?

LANDON: Oh, yeah. When it totally takes you over? Big physical changes take place. You know, your pupils dilate— even getting ready, especially when I used to do live television. I can remember standing in a soundstage before a scene I knew I was gonna kill 'em with. I can remember one case in point, at "Playhouse 90" called "Project: Immortality," where I played Lee J. Cobb's son. I had this big scene coming up, and I couldn't wait. I was trying to control all this adrenaline that's going, and I looked up at the lights at the station, CBS Television City, and they had huge streamers coming off. My pupils were so dilated, I had so much adrenaline going, I couldn't wait for this thing to start. You get great release after a big emotional scene, whether it's tears or anger or whatever it is. Big release. You feel like you've had a big massage. You know, just limp.

I know other actors go through that. That's why it's so important that you don't make the staging so complicated and the camera so difficult that mechanically you screw up. You know, if the actor screws up, the actor screws up. And a lot of times I'll pick 'em and make them go again right away anyway. I'll never cut the camera. I'll say, "I don't care about that line." Because these things are not automatic. They don't happen take after take after take after take. So give 'em the biggest break you can.

If they have the heavy end of the scene do 'em first, then do 'em with two cameras, and make sure that you're doing it in a way that the operator *can't* screw up. Because nothing makes a guy feel so like hell as when the dam is bursting and he's feeling so good about the performance, and then someone says, "Jeez, I didn't get it!"

How many of those do you have in you?

LANDON: [*Groans*] How many do you have in you? It's tough! Very tough!

You're in a situation that is fascinating for a lot of people because you can draw on those moments of inspiration on so many creative levels: producing, directing, acting, and writing. Are there occasions when all three or four have combined in a creation of yours that just really put you up there? "This is something I wrote, I performed in, I'm acting in, I have control over, and it will live forever"?

LANDON: [*Laughs*] Well, no, that I never feel. I've gotta be honest with you: no.

Or, shall we say, that you got great momentary satisfaction from?

LANDON: Oh, sure! Great momentary satisfaction. But I've never done anything that [*laughs*] should live forever. I've just done some nice things. I've done some good things.

"This is not an infinite place we're living on, you know. It's nice to talk about outer space and all that other stuff, but it's gonna be a long time before we find another place to live, if we can ever do that. This place is packed! It wasn't meant to be this way."

MICHAEL LANDON

13

CITIZEN LANDON

MICHAEL LANDON'S GIFT TO THE WORLD WILL FOREVER remain the compelling humanism of his work. Aided by a Minnesota farmer's integrity or a probationary angel's mission, we were reminded in Landon's shows how good it could feel to be human in the best sense of the word. We could contend with droughts and blight, poverty and pride, disease and despair, and yet acknowledge it all with a dignity born of flesh and blood and spirit. For Michael did more than chronicle human suffering and frustration. He dramatized in his stories the obstinate dreams fostered by bitter struggle in this life and the triumphs that faith alone can achieve. He moved us to heed the heart and to consider our conscience. The entertainment of his vehicles brought us to laughter and tears, reason and realizations. If there was an escape route that his shows provided us with, it was perhaps the escape that brought us back to our own unabashed idealism.

Michael believed deeply in an individual's responsibility to strive for greater and active enlightenment. It began with self-realization and inevitably led to personal and public service. As a family man, he had a tremendous concern for the Earth his children and grandchildren would inherit. And he could be as forthright in expressing his personal views on pollution, the tremendous waste of our natural resources, and other human obscenities as he was in dramatizing them for a television audience.

Several "Highway to Heaven" episodes directly addressed the environmental hazards that now imperil all of mankind. One of the most compelling stories was titled "Birds of a Feather"; it dealt with the perils of groundwater pollution caused by industrial waste. That episode also happened to mark the professional debut of Maureen Flannigan, who was only eleven years old at the time and went on to star in her own television series, "Out of This World," which ran for four seasons. Maureen recalls the excitement of working with Michael Landon as an opportunity that led to a greater personal as well as professional self-realization.

MAUREEN FLANNIGAN: I was eleven years old at the time my mother took me to work on the "Highway to Heaven" series. I was so nervous because it was really the first big theatrical thing I had ever done. As it turned out, I only had one line to do on a hill with some other kids, but I kept rehearsing it over and over in my mind! I had loved the show "Little House on the Prairie" and was very excited to meet Michael Landon.

I remember when I saw him, he had this tremendous mane of hair, and he was like this big kid cracking jokes and playing around. He had so much energy, and I later had a chance to play tennis with him at a tournament. The story line of the episode I appeared in dealt with groundwater pollution, and confronting this issue in my work did a great deal to raise my own awareness and concern for our environment.

As I've grown older, I've begun to realize more and more how necessary it is to be an activist in improving the problems of our society. You can't just sit around and think that someone else is going to do it for you. What I think we need are real reforms based on a genuine commitment to heal our world, and like Michael, I want to be someone who tries to help bring about those reforms.

As A CITIZEN OF THE PLANET, LANDON DID MORE THAN pay his taxes and cosmetically endorse public relations campaigns. He gave generously of himself, both financially and through personal active support of those causes that touched his conscience and his heart. One organization to which both Michael Landon and his wife Cindy especially opened their hearts was Free Arts for Abused Children. FAAC is a California nonprofit corporation that introduces creative arts activities to victims of child abuse as outlets through which they can grow.

Both Elda Unger, president emeritus of FAAC, and Barbara Lashenick, director, worked closely with the Landon family in coordinating numerous functions and events of the organization.

BARBARA LASHENICK: The circumstances that brought Michael and me together are different from what brought Michael and Free Arts together. Elda Unger, who is the president of Free Arts, has a beautiful home in Malibu next to Johnny Carson's home. Michael Landon was there; they were using her home to film something. And no one walks into Elda's home without becoming a member of Free Arts, knowing about Free Arts, and making a lifelong commitment to Free Arts!

So, she brought Michael in and made him aware of it and became friendly with him and Cindy and asked him to host Moonlight Roundup in the summer. That is how our relationship began. He also did a public service announcement for us, and that public service broadcast eventually brought an overwhelming response from people who wanted to help Free

Arts because they had seen Michael Landon. They couldn't remember what they saw, but they wrote down the number because it was Michael Landon's picture on the screen saying, "Support this. Dial the number and call." He had *tremendous* drawing power.

When someone comes forward, especially someone of the caliber of Michael Landon, and can do so much by opening his mouth and supporting something—I just thought he was the greatest thing since dark chocolate!

I think that Michael's own troubled past as a child, which we knew about, led him to support this organization. Free Arts functions upon the basic ethic that art heals, utilizing such creative outlets as sports and acting in art to help bring children out of their confusion and hurt and anger and to emotionally adjust to society. Those outlets were certainly a part of Michael's background, and that helped him heal his wounds. He never lost sight of where he came from. And when he looked at a hurt child, he wanted to heal that child.

ELDA UNGER: You asked me how Free Arts was fortunate enough to meet Michael. That was so synchronistic. Three days before I had actually met him, I had been talking to some of the peo-

ple on our executive board about the many celebrities who were helping us. And I said,
"There's one person. If we could only have Michael Landon. Some of the values with which he
has come across and his shows have been so
wholesome and family-oriented, he would just
be perfect! If we could only get Michael Landon
involved with Free Arts."

I think it was about two or three days later
when he walked into this house because they
had planned on using the kitchen portion for
shooting some segment for a project he was involved with. We very often will rent out a room
in the house for a commercial or for some scene
in a movie. It turned out that the company had
contacted my husband for this arrangement.

I had no knowledge of this, and I walked in
and saw Michael Landon! Of course he was
trapped in the house for the entire day, filming,
and that gave me a chance to really tell him
about Free Arts. He was so responsive and inter-
ested in the fact that we were an organization
that helped abused and neglected children and
that we reached them through the arts. He just
really tuned in to the whole concept of the heal-
ing effect through the arts and through being
creative because he was so tremendously creative.

Shortly before Michael became ill, we
brought children from two residential care facil-

ities over to their home for a Free Arts Day. Every month we designate a Free Arts Day for a residential care facility. We'll be going in the morning, spend the entire day in various activities for the children including artwork, like painting T-shirts or making masks, and doing a "music machine" where people sing along with a recorded band. It's like a three-ring circus of the arts.

Michael and Cindy really wanted to do a Free Arts Day, and we were able to do this at their home in February of 1991. It was really an amazing thing to watch. Michael was there making T-shirts with the kids, and Leslie, his daughter, who was there along with her husband, and Chris, Michael's son, were really into it. They had this big, spacious place for the kids to run around in, and Michael and the whole Landon family worked with these kids.

Michael had purchased pizza, and there he was passing out pizza and salad to all the kids. He was having such a terrific time, as was the whole family. That is one of my most beautiful memories of watching Michael with the kids and really providing the whole day for them. He was so accessible. I saw some of the staff workers from some of the facilities go up to talk with him somewhat hesitantly, and he just immediately made them feel good. It was a genuine concern, and I believed everybody felt that.

OVERPOPULATION WAS ANOTHER ISSUE ABOUT WHICH Michael had particularly strong feelings. A conservationist at heart, he had been to Africa on photographic safari and was fascinated by the vast regions where wildlife has survived and flourished for millennia guided solely by what seems to be the irrevocable intelligence of primitive nature itself.

~

LANDON: You know, you always tend to think about what it's gonna be like for your great grandchildren, your grandchildren, down the line, and it'll be impossible at the rate we're going. Double the population in the world every twenty-five years; the Earth's not getting any larger. We don't know what to do with the pollutants now.

It's not enough just to clean up our act and get rid of some chlorofluorocarbons. We all have to be honest about it. We have to raise the poverty level of people all over the world. People don't have a lot of kids when they have money. It's only when you're just flat out below the poverty level and dead poor that you have a lot of kids for no reason—because it doesn't cost you any more to have any more kids. I mean, if you live in Ethiopia, it doesn't cost you anything to have twelve kids as opposed to four kids. I mean, you're used to dying anyway. What you're hoping is that when you're old maybe some of these twelve will be alive so they can bring you a cup of water, because you can't get it yourself. You're gonna be too sick. So they just keep having kids.

It's been the history of civilization that, the more that you get rid of that poverty, people then begin thinking about how many children they're going to have. If you live outside, it isn't crowded. If you live in a house, there's only *x* amount of places to sleep.

And we have to stop believing that it's some religious thing that man wrote about. I mean, God didn't say that contraception is bad. Man did, because man wanted to have more church members. It's true. There's no two ways about it.

So there's this planet that your children are going to be inhabiting and, after you're gone, their children. You'd like them to have enough to live a good life on.

LANDON: Absolutely. See, we're so polarized now. If you say anything, for instance "We can't keep allowing millions of people to come across the border illegally from Mexico," the minute people start talking about that, it becomes "prejudice." Well, it has absolutely nothing to do with prejudice. What it has to do with is all of the people coming across the border who do not speak the language, who have no jobs waiting for them. There isn't going to be any employment—what are they going to do?

Instead of spending our money helping the Mexican government, helping that country pull itself by its bootstraps, we should be getting more open press so that people can find out how much ripping off is being done. No one rips off anybody like their own. I mean, no one rips off black people like black people, and no one rips off Mexican people like Mexican people, because they're the ones that can get away with it!

We can talk about all the problems of the ozone and this and that and everything else, and none of that is worth discussing unless we begin to face the overpopulation of this planet, which nobody does!

This is not an infinite place we're living on, you know. It's nice to talk about outer space and all that other stuff, but it's gonna be a long time before we find another place to live, if we can *ever* do that. This place is packed! It wasn't meant to be this way.

It was terrific that God gave us all of the gifts to be able to create the medicines that we've created. But all the people that in nature just die, so that the balance of nature can be kept, don't die anymore.

You said it wasn't meant to be this way. How do you think it was meant to be?

LANDON: Well, if I had the master plan, I think probably God must have figured that if you had enough knowledge to cure these diseases and to have these medical breakthroughs that man has been able to accomplish, at the same time you would be bright enough to realize that you cannot continue growing in numbers the way you're growing, that you've gotta put a halt to it.

Like nature puts a halt to it on its own. If you go to Africa, for instance, let's say you've got one dry season and another dry season. You see all the gazelles running around, right? Except if it's a *dry* season, they are not procreating. You don't see a male gazelle with his little harem of twenty or thirty females.

All the females stay over here, and all the males stay over there. And the males have what appears to be a homosexual relationship of game playing, of snuggling and nudging. The females do the same thing, but they don't have any babies! Because there isn't any water, there isn't gonna be any food, *and they know it*. So I guess gazelles are smarter than we are! [*Laughs*]

"I think it's very presumptuous for anyone to think that they should be remembered by anybody else except their family. I mean in this little short space of time that we're here, over the great thousands of years that are gonna pass, who's really gonna be remembered? And for what reason?"

MICHAEL LANDON

14

THE LEGACY

MICHAEL LANDON'S IMAGE AS A FAMILY MAN IS ONE OF the truest and most enduring projections of both his personal and professional identity. Michael had, in essence, two families: his own wife and children and the people with whom he worked. In a moving testament of their great love for him, members of both unions participated in a special television tribute to Michael's memory shortly after his death.

The commemoration was a poignant result of the confluence of two distinctly different passions in Landon's life: his family and his work. Much of our conversation revealed his constant striving to reconcile these two diverse factors as well as his own dichotomous traits: a love of solitude and a natural gregariousness and deep capacity to love.

He got married for the first time to Dodie Fraser in 1956 and adopted her son, Mark, and then the couple adopted another son, Josh. In 1962 Michael divorced Dodie, married Lynn Noe, and adopted her daughter, Cheryl. During their nineteen-year marriage, Michael and Lynn had four more children: Leslie, Michael Jr., Shawna, and Christopher. In 1983 he was married for the third time, to Cindy Clerico. The mother of his youngest children, Jennifer and Sean, she was at Michael's bedside when he died.

Michael found great joy in all of the loving energy and activity that a clan of nine children can bring. Yet he also found fulfillment in an inner chamber of dreams, where no one could follow. It was an inviolable sanctuary that allowed him to find refuge from home in work and alternately seek refuge from work in home.

"I don't think it was ever satisfied," remarked Harry Flynn when I stated this opinion. "I don't think he ever resolved it. The two were inextricably mixed, because Michael Jr. worked on 'Highway' every day as one of the cinematography crew. Although he never brought the work home, several of the kids had been on 'Little House' and were familiar with it.

"And the crew was family, so they would be in touch in the evenings just as friends. There was a spillover, but home stayed home when he went to work because it would have been impossible if he hadn't made some differentiation."

~

Much of the public perceives you as a patriarch because of your television image—the Pa Ingalls thing and the company you've created—and because of your own large family. Do you believe that your great professional success harmonized with your success as a family man?

LANDON: [*Considers the question for several moments*] That's a really complicated one. Everybody wants to get married one time and stay married one time, and I guess you can say that I could look probably very unsuccessful as a family man because I've had three marriages. [*Another pause*]

But I have a tremendous closeness with all of my children. And I think the nature of my business is—or maybe everybody's business, I don't know—but being a celebrity is different from just being successful. There's a lot of very successful businesspeople who can go anywhere, and nothing special is expected or demanded of them. It's different with somebody in the public eye. You know people say, "How does a couple who have two people in the business get along well?" I'm not so sure that it wouldn't be easier perhaps for the wife of a successful actor to be a successful actress herself. Celebrity does strange things . . .

~

During the course of your career I've noticed certain summits. I can look back and see certain periodic challenges that you created for yourself and thrust yourself into and came away winning.

LANDON: Yeah. Well, it's just moxie. I mean, you gotta have some moxie. Otherwise all those moments would have passed.

Do you see that ahead of you? Are you going to do that again?

LANDON: What, the moxie? I'll always have moxie. Yeah, I'll always have it. I mean that's something I owe my parents. I owe both my mother and father a great deal in terms of what my legacy was from them. It isn't particularly one that I'd like to give to my kids, in terms of pain and seeing a family like the one I had. My family was not the kind a kid would like to grow up in.

But on the other hand, God compensates. You receive gifts from pain. Good comes out of bad. Moxie is one of my gifts. My open emotionalism is one of my gifts. I probably wouldn't have had those things if I had come from a very comfortable, everything's-OK family.

You're into your third marriage, so obviously there's been a real struggle that you've gone through to attain a certain peace of mind or joy that may have eluded you in the past. Have you achieved that now?

LANDON: [*Reflects*] Gee, I don't know. [*Suddenly brightens*] Oh, yeah! I guess I achieved it. The first time, I got married—and my first wife knows we shouldn't have gotten married—because I couldn't tell my oldest son, Mark, who is my adopted son (he was seven years old at the time), that I didn't want to marry his mother. It's what happens to you when you've just turned nineteen. You're not quite as straightforward as you should be at that time.

My second marriage was nineteen years. A long time. But with two people who were quite different when they got married and continued to drift apart in terms of life-styles and what was important—I was kind of a blue-collar husband married to a woman who should have been with, I think, a very big top executive or someone who was *king* or something! [*Laughs*]

So now your wife's name is Cindy, right? And you're happy?

LANDON: Yeah. And my kids really care for her, which is great.

You know, the anger is over. There's always gonna be anger when you get divorced. Not from your little kids usually, but with the older ones—especially if you have older kids. But if someone is just basically so damn nice, pretty soon, after a period of time, even though people want to have anger, they can't have it anymore.

Cindy and I both knew going in that we were going to have to understand that it was gonna be there. Even when they pretended that it wasn't. I finally told them, "I'd really like to see some anger here, you know, instead of bullshit, which is what I'm getting. Don't give me phony smiles when I know that isn't the way you're feeling. I can handle that. Just don't be phony with me. That's like lying. And that's always been our big thing. Don't lie. *Don't lie to me!* I'd rather have a terrific argument and clear the air! If you don't want to come around for a while, don't come around. It's OK."

She sounds like a very wise woman.

LANDON: Yeah! It's worked out great. Jeez, I call her all the time for advice. And my kids, they're always on the phone with Cin', they chat for a while . . .

Is there a strong nurturing aspect to her personality?

LANDON: *Yes!* Yes. She's a terrific mother. I mean really very dedicated, which was something I had to get used to. It was in a way not easy for me. Jealous of that. I got a little angry about that myself. I mean where was my time? It was all being spent on little kids.

With my second wife there was basically no time spent with them, which again is more, I guess, an aristocratic way of bringing up kids. That's what nannies are for. They make breakfast, they take them to school, they do the homework with them—they do these things. You hire people, and they do those things. It's really not right. It's not good. But it's another way of doin' it. I just don't think it's as good.

In an interview I saw you do with "Entertainment Tonight," you said it pretty well: There are no strangers in your home when

you come home. You have an image as a family man. You have
many children, and they all seemed devoted to you.

LANDON: They're all very different. One son, Josh, is the
kind of guy that likes to be as far away from a lot of people
as possible, and he's a very low-key guy. Not an aggressive
kind of a guy at all. Some of my kids are very aggressive in
terms of business and working, but they all have in common—they're all kind people. I mean, my kids are all kind.

Do you see an extension of yourself in each and every one of
them?

LANDON: Oh, sure. I think so.

You have a code of honor, obviously—ethics and ideals. Despite
the variety of their personalities, do you see a consistency in that
essential character?

LANDON: Yeah, and I see them as they grow up doing a lot
of the same things I did, making the same mistakes. I
think if you've made enough in your life, as I have, it's
probably easier to understand those kinds of mistakes in
your kids. I mean if you were a perfect kid—I guess there
are some. I talk to parents, and they have them. I was just
not one of those kids.

I wasn't an easy kid. I got into a *lot* of trouble when I
was a kid, and I failed school because I thought I'd be more
popular failing school. I got into a lot of fights. I mean I

never went on my senior trip in high school because I was supposed to be incorrigible and there would be a problem if I went. I graduated 299th out of 301. That's no thrill for anybody's family. [*Laughs*]

But on the other hand, in a way I guess it kind of helps you with your kids, because you see so much of yourself. The stuff you try to get away with, the stuff you do out of anger, the stuff you do because you want to get along with other kids. I have a couple of children who should have gotten much better grades than they got, but they're the children of Michael Landon.

They tend to get a lot of crap from other kids, because children tend to view me as a "Mr. Goody-Two Shoes" religious leader of some kind, like I'm the real square guy. Which I'm not. My kids know that. But in order to show them that they're not like that, to show the others, they would tend to do things and clown around and get in trouble, just to be one of the regular guys or gals.

Well, most of your kids are adults now, right? They're grown up.

LANDON: Yeah, but a lot of them went through it.

And so, at this point, you guys are all friends, I take it.

LANDON: Oh, sure. Oh God, yeah!

Would you consider that to be the mainstay of the joy in your life? You're in your element at work, and you love your job. But then there's that other part where you go home when your job is over. You leave it behind. So I got the feeling you were drawing on two distinct wellsprings for your joy and that they're different and separate.

LANDON: If something goes bad at work, so what! I mean anything that has to do with illness or pain or emotional problems with people that are family—those are tough things. Tough things are not at work. I mean, shit, you correct those things. They're easy to fix right away.

You once made a two-part show that you did on "Little House" called "The Legacy." At the very end you walked up to your wife on the show and said, "You're right. The children are my legacy. I don't need anything else." Well, that was the character, but I know you need more than children for your legacy. But do you—

LANDON: Oh, I don't think you do. I think that's the only legacy people need: the knowledge that when you're ready to leave this place you've left behind a bunch of young people who are actually going to be good for this planet. They're gonna do good things. The world's gonna be better because they're around. That makes you feel good.

But whatever else we do—whether it be in this business or in the writing of books or the painting of paintings—I think it's very presumptuous for anyone to think that they should be remembered by anybody else except their family. I mean in this little short space of time that we're here, over the great thousands of years that are gonna pass, who's really gonna be remembered? And for what reason?

So it's a human bequeathal you're talking about.

LANDON: Oh, yeah! You know, you hope that way, way, way down the line, if you have the kind of family where everybody talks, the oldest person can then continue to hand down the knowledge of the family and the caring and so forth. That's good stuff.

AFTERWORD

Crew members bundled up in windbreakers, many
of them wearing mesh-back caps, sat randomly
around long plank tables . . . Most of them had come
a long way with Michael, many of them through
three television series and now, it seemed, into a
fourth.

15
Us

IN LATE 1990, SHORTLY AFTER THESE TAPED CONVERSA-
tions, Michael Landon's production company did indeed
become an affiliate of Columbia Broadcasting. The "big
changes" he had mentioned regarding his career were
initiated with the development of a pilot for a proposed
new television series to be called "Us," based on a story
Michael had written.

A new "boss" and another show. In view of the reluc-
tance Michael had expressed weeks earlier, I was somewhat surprised although pleased by the news. Michael was
back in harness and at the height of his creative powers.

His production company had relocated to the familiar
Culver City surroundings on Washington Boulevard. The
former MGM studio that housed it had gone through

breathtaking changes over the past few years. Since "Little House on the Prairie" had closed, MGM had been supplanted on the lot by Lorimar Pictures, had engaged in a brief flirtation with Warner Brothers, and by the close of 1990 had been taken over by Columbia Pictures (now Sony Pictures).

The studio itself was undergoing a partial face-lift, and the tentative company signs displayed at the gates were oddly symbolic of a somewhat unsettling transitional period of mergers and takeovers. As a film community Culver City seemed to undergo many of these cosmetic changes as well.

Culver Studios received a fresh coat of paint and an accompanying new system of streetlights. Down the street and within the shadow of Columbia Studios the old Culver City city hall was condemned and eventually razed. The wrecking ball swung on Big Ed's as well, as landmarks vanished and parking lots appeared.

It seemed to me that television programming itself was (and is) going through a strange metamorphosis. It was the age of the half-hour sitcom. One-hour family dramas of the quality that Landon had produced appeared nearly extinct, kept alive only by the grace of syndication. The news of his proposed return to primetime television, then, brightened this picture considerably. I could feel the renaissance emerging. Landon wound up production on Us, a television feature film he had written as a pilot for a proposed series, toward the end of December 1990. I was invited to the set of the show on its final day of shooting.

The company had been filming in an old warehouse off Warner Avenue adjacent to an industrial park in Culver City.

It was around 9:30 in the morning and raining when I pulled the car up to the lowered wooden arm of the parking gate. A crew member looked at me inquiringly. "Michael Landon Productions?" I queried. The fellow smiled and inserted his card. "You said the magic words," he replied as the gate arm saluted upward.

I saw the familiar honey wagons and catering truck clustered alongside the old building. A few wooden steps led up to the soundstage, where a momentarily dark warning light stood like a sentinel at the half-opened door. I entered the dim barnlike room and walked over to the stage. Michael was seated in his director's chair, intently reviewing the script.

The set had been constructed to represent a modest apartment interior, and I walked curiously around and through the various partitions, watching the setup and reluctant to disturb Landon. A few moments later, however, he looked up and smiled. We shook hands and he lit a cigarette.

"Another show. That's wonderful," I said. Michael nodded somewhat abstractly and mentioned the demographics of his research regarding the series' possible chances for success. It promised to be another hit, and I found the premise intriguing.

The story centered around an ex-convict (played by Landon) who after eighteen years in prison is found innocent of his alleged crime. Released from confinement, he faces a difficult reunion with both his father (Barney Martin) and a teenage son (Casey Peterson), whom he has not seen since infancy. The often bittersweet communication dilemmas of father-son relationships were a recurring theme in a number of Michael's projects.

It mirrored a great deal of the frustration he had experienced in his own unhappy childhood regarding his father, for whom Michael had a wistful if somewhat disenchanted affection. Throughout much his life Michael played the role of strong father figure to both his family and his crew. But I think that there was always within him something of the prodigal son, who yearned for paternal approval, as well.

Interestingly enough, the role Landon portrayed in "Us" was the middle figure, who was both father and son in a drama of three generations of guys. We discussed the concept of the show between setups, and it was evident that he cared deeply about the project.

I will always be grateful for the invitation to visit the set on the day Landon wrapped Us, for it turned out to be my one opportunity to watch him direct. The crew was absolutely the friendliest group of people I had ever met in television production, and they indeed seemed to be "the best people in town" at what they did.

"It's fun to come to work," the wardrobe mistress effused to me once during a break. Where had I heard that before? It was tremendously impressive to see the obvious great confidence Landon's crew had in his professional ability. They worked with the precise synchronization of long accustomedness, along with an enthusiasm that seemed to anticipate Michael's creative spontaneity.

Most fascinating of all, however, was the compelling presence of Michael himself. He was quietly intent while working—competent, focused, and flexible. He never shouted. If problems arose regarding a shot (and a few came up during the day), he seemed simply to correct them. He had a handle on both the spirit and the mechanics of what he was doing.

There was one particular incident that especially impressed me. While directing a particular scene, Michael and the crew ran into a problem with the position of his camera. The scene as originally written called for Barney Martin to open the low refrigerator door and take out some food to begin dinner. Because of the cramped quarters of the set, the limited room made maneuvering the camera for an effective shot difficult.

The scene was tried one way and then another with frustrating results. Michael pondered the dilemma for a few moments in silence. Finally he spoke up. "I know what we'll do," he announced. "We'll rewrite and have you open the freezer door and take out some ice cream." Rather than letting this small problem grow into a big one, as a matter of course Michael made the adjustment right there and then, and the scene went flawlessly.

Michael understood his people. He could at the most astonishing times deliver a line that would break up everyone around him. On that particular day he was responsible for a lot of hilarity on the set. Gene Trindl had been assigned to shoot a number of publicity stills for the show and was busily arranging the principals for their poses. Costars Barney Martin and Casey Peterson cooperated, but Michael seemed bent on using the session to deliver a nonstop monologue of bawdy jokes. It still breaks me up to see those photos and know the cause of the smiles on the guys' faces.

We broke for lunch around noon, and Maury Dexter, who had worked as Michael's assistant director for years, pushed me into the grub line, exhorting me to get a steak "any way I wanted it." I took my plate and pitched in at a table along with Harry Flynn, Dexter, and Gene Trindl. Barney Martin sat beside me, comfortably digesting his meal and thoughts of the upcoming hiatus. Everyone seemed to feel that they were involved in yet another hit show, for after all, when had it ever been otherwise?

That break carried all the feeling of a company picnic. Crew members bundled up in windbreakers, many of them wearing mesh-back caps, sat randomly around long plank tables and joined in the informal and unstructured conversation characteristic of people who have worked together for a very long time. It was a comfortable and earthy community. Most of them had come a long way with Michael, many of them through three television series and now, it seemed, into a fourth.

I remember thinking back to that one evening five years earlier, when I had first by chance encountered the same crew set up on that Culver City street by Big Ed's.

Of them all, I could recall only Michael and the man I now know was Kent McCray being there. But I was a stranger then, standing on the sidelines curiously watching this imposing unit of people functioning so harmoniously under the direction of the denim-shirted, long-haired boss who merely stood there whistling softly to himself.

As the lunch hour wound down, cast and crew, for the most part unbidden by the assistant director, automatically resumed their duties. Lighting fixtures were moved, cameras repositioned, monitors wheeled in, and microphones tested. Actors checked their makeup and glanced at their lines. Michael reappeared and moved unobtrusively among them, pacing back and forth, speaking his lines aloud to himself.

Dick Lilley, Michael's stand-in, walked over to the coffee table where I stood. "Last day," he said and smiled. He sounded almost regretful. I looked on inquiringly as Michael's retake man, Hank Brissinger, checked something with his earphones. Noticing my curiosity, he slipped the earphones off and handed them to me. "Here," he invited. "Have a listen."

Gratefully I put the headpiece on and listened intently. Suddenly all the marvelous sounds of the production came to me, making all of the distant action on the crowded set several feet away seem immediate and intimate. I thanked Hank and handed back the earphones. "It all works, doesn't it?" I asked, and he nodded. "Mike makes it work," he replied.

Pamela Roylance, who had worked in the final season

of "Little House on the Prairie," had been kind enough to lend me her album of photographs taken of the cast and crew of that show. I had brought the book with me onto the set, thinking that some of the folks would enjoy the memories. During the seven hours or so that I was there, the book of photos drew nearly everyone: Kent and Susan McCray, Maury Dexter, Haskell Boggs, and nearly every other crew member. It was so popular that I eventually just left the album on a card table.

Only Michael remained distant, and that made me a little nervous. Was he sore about the distraction? Finally I walked up to where he was seated and pointed back toward the album. "Your crew seems to be like a big family over there looking at those pictures," I said. Michael nodded. "Yeah, it's cute isn't it?" he replied.

I hesitated. "I hope you don't mind that I brought it." Michael stubbed out his cigarette and grinned. "Shit no!" he declared. About a half hour later, I noticed him walk over to the table and begin paging through the album. Coming upon a photo of himself with gray hair, he guffawed and said loudly, "Who's that white-haired bastard?" A few pages later he came across a shot of actor Dabbs Greer, who had played Reverend Alden in "Little House," dressed in clerical garb and giving the photographer the finger.

A hearty laugh came from Michael in response to Greer's mischievous irreverence. "This guy," he remarked, "has the greatest sense of humor!" A moment later he turned the page, and a photograph of his daughter, Leslie, smiling in costume, appeared. His jovial air evaporated, to be replaced with a soft, fond exclamation: "Aw!"

I think a lot of Michael Landon as a man was epitomized in that little incident: his shyness, aggressiveness, humor, sentiment, and kindness. Michael had sensed my uneasiness. He made the gesture to show his acceptance.

Michael wrapped the show at about five o'clock in the afternoon. As was his custom, he thanked everyone, announced the completion of another fine endeavor by Haskell Boggs, and led the applause as the venerable cinematographer with two artificial hips gamely shuffled off the set.

I gathered my materials, retrieved the album, and walked up to Michael, who stood talking to Kent. "Drive carefully!" he said and shook my hand. It was to be the last time I saw him.

On September 20, 1991, shortly after Michael's death on July 1, CBS aired *Us*, the pilot feature for the television series he would never make. It was Michael Landon's final film.

16

EPILOGUE

SEVERAL WEEKS AFTER MY VISIT TO THE SET, WHEN I heard of Michael Landon's illness, I enclosed a couple of items in a manila envelope and took it to Harry Flynn. "Would you see that Michael gets this?" I asked. Harry nodded kindly and replied, "I'll bring it to him later today."

Within the envelope I had included a vintage Green Lantern comic with a cover depicting the great superhero that Michael, as a kid, had emulated battling a force of evil. Along with it was a short letter that recalled our conversations and the inspiration of his friendship. The letter read in part:

> Dear Michael,
> You once spoke to me about "living the dream."
> We both know that many of your best dreams

and challenges are yet to be lived and that their fulfillment is a matter of destiny.

There is one personal aspiration, long cherished, that I would confide to you. It is the hope of one day soon placing in your hand the published realization of the insights we have shared from the compelling expression of your philosophy. And to say with pride and gratitude, "We have done this, my friend."

It was a simple communication in which I hoped to make it clear that I expected to share with him one day the pride of friendship's endeavor. But then, I still do.

THE WORKS OF
MICHAEL LANDON

TELEVISION

AS A REGULAR

"Bonanza," NBC, 1959–73

"Little House on the Prairie," NBC, 1974–82

"Highway to Heaven," NBC, 1984–89

AS PERFORMER

"Telephone Time: The Mystery of Caspar Hauser," CBS,
 1956

"Wire Service: High Adventure," ABC, 1956

"DuPont Theater: The Man From St. Paul," ABC, 1957

"Telephone Time: Fight for the Title," ABC, 1957

"General Electric Theater: Too Good with a Gun," CBS,
 1957

"Schlitz Playhouse of Stars: The Restless Gun," CBS,
 1957

"Tales of Wells Fargo: Gunshot Messenger," NBC, 1957
"The Court of Last Resort: The Forbes-Carroll Case,"
    NBC, 1957
"Tales of Wells Fargo: The Kid," NBC, 1957
"Cheyenne: White Warrior," ABC, 1957
"Schlitz Playhouse of Stars: Hands of the Enemy," CBS,
    1957
"The Adventures of Jim Bowie: Deputy Sheriff," ABC,
    1958
"Goodyear Theatre: The Giant Step," NBC, 1958
"Schlitz Playhouse of Stars: Way of the West," CBS, 1958
"Tales of Wells Fargo: Sam Bass," NBC, 1958
"Wanted Dead or Alive: The Martin Poster," CBS, 1958
"The Texan: The Hemp Tree," CBS, 1958
"Dick Powell's Zane Grey Theater: Living Is a Lonesome
    Thing," CBS, 1959
"Wanted Dead or Alive: The Legend," CBS, 1959
"Tombstone Territory: The Man from Brewster," ABC,
    1959
"Playhouse 90: Project Immortality," CBS, 1959
"Johnny Staccato: The Naked Truth," NBC, 1959
"Here's Hollywood," NBC, 1960
"Your First Impression," NBC, 1962
"Your First Impression," NBC, 1963
"Stump the Stars," CBS, 1963
"Truth or Consequences," NBC, 1964
"You Don't Say," NBC, 1964
"Vacation Playhouse: Luke and the Tenderfoot," CBS,
    1965
"Hullabaloo," NBC, 1965

Red, NBC, 1970
Mitzi and a Hundred Guys, CBS, 1975
"General Electric's All-Star Anniversary," ABC, 1978
"Little House: A New Beginning: Home Again," NBC,
     1983

As Producer-Director and Performer
Little House on the Prairie (series pilot), NBC, 1974
"Little House on the Prairie" (series), NBC, 1974-82
The Loneliest Runner, NBC, 1976
Love Is Forever, NBC, 1983
Little House: Look Back to Yesterday, NBC, 1983
Little House: Bless All the Dear Children, NBC, 1984
Little House: The Last Farewell, NBC, 1984
Sam's Son, NBC, 1984
"Highway to Heaven" (series), NBC, 1984-89
Where Pigeons Go to Die, NBC, 1990
Us (series pilot), CBS, 1991

As Writer-Producer-Director
Love Story: Love Came Laughing, NBC, 1973
"Father Murphy" (series), NBC, 1981-82
"Little House: A New Beginning" (series), NBC, 1982-83

    Film
I Was a Teen-age Werewolf, 1957
God's Little Acre, 1958
High School Confidential!, 1958
The Legend of Tom Dooley, 1959